"What Choice Do I Have?"

READING, WRITING, AND SPEAKING ACTIVITIES
TO EMPOWER STUDENTS

Terry Patrick Bigelow and Michael J. Vokoun

Foreword by Jeffrey N. Golub

HEINEMANN
Portsmouth, NH

Heinemann
A division of Reed Elsevier Inc.
361 Hanover Street
Portsmouth, NH 03801–3912
www.heinemann.com

Offices and agents throughout the world

60596086

Library of Congress Cataloging-in-Publication Data
Bigelow, Terry Patrick.
    What choice do I have? : reading, writing, and speaking activities to empower students / Terry Patrick Bigelow and Michael J. Vokoun ; foreword by Jeffrey N. Golub.
        p. cm.
    Includes bibliographical references and index.
    ISBN 0-325-00714-4 (alk. paper)
    1. Active learning. 2. Student-centered learning. I. Vokoun, Michael J. II. Title.

LB1027.23.B55 2005
371.39—dc22   2005012515

Editor: James Strickland
Production: Vicki Kasabian
Cover design: Night & Day Design
Typesetter: Tom Allen, Pear Graphic Design
Manufacturing: Jamie Carter

Printed in the United States of America on acid-free paper
09 08 07 06 05 VP 1 2 3 4 5

This book is dedicated to our wives, who make life worthwhile,
and to Jeffrey N. Golub, who taught us when to dismount and when to ride.

CONTENTS

FOREWORD

This is a book about making *student engagement* happen. Engagement is different from motivation. If one needs to *motivate* students to complete the task at hand, then there is a problem: it implies that the task by itself is not very exciting, that the students do not readily see the value or pertinence involved. If they did see it, then you wouldn't have to prod and persuade and *motivate* them to do it, would you? They would simply dive in and become engaged in the work without first asking, "Do we have to?" "Is this for a grade?" or "Is this going to be on the test?"

In my two English methods texts, *Activities for an Interactive Classroom* (1994) and *Making Learning Happen* (2000), I emphasized four crucial principles, procedures, and practices that, if integrated into the structure and design of one's lessons and instructional activities, would make student engagement happen: (1) students are performing with language; (2) students' own talk is used as a vehicle for learning; (3) students communicate to real audiences for real purposes; (4) the teacher functions in the classroom as a designer and director of instruction.

But now, with the publication of this remarkably insightful and illuminating text, authors Terry Bigelow and Michael Vokoun identify and describe a fifth element involved in making student engagement happen—and it is every bit as important as the others; it is, in the authors' own words, "providing students with some control and choice over their learning."

The authors make a compelling case for the importance of choice in the design of one's classroom activities. Allowing students choices in the how and the when, and in the form and the format of their language performances and their portfolios and projects promotes a sense of ownership. It is this sense of ownership, in turn, that leads students to become engaged and to care about their coursework.

This is not a book to be simply read. Rather, it is to be *used*. And the authors make it easy for you to do so. Each chapter features first a description of the activity or project; then we go into the authors' classrooms and get anecdotes about how (and how well) the activity worked when it was actually run. The next sections, How to Make It Happen, Adaptations, and Q & A, enable you, in James Britton's words, to "assimilate the task to your own understanding"; that is, to shape the instruction and procedures in ways that fit your own teaching style.

This, then, is one of the reasons I like this book so much: it promises to make teachers' instruction and students' learning new and improved by extending the interactive classroom to include student choice, thereby making students even more active participants in their own learning.

But there is another, even more important, reason I am attracted to this book, and it has to do with the authors themselves: Michael and Terry are former students of mine at the University of South Florida who have gone on to become master teachers. I taught them to drive, and they have now become driving instructors themselves. I look at what they can do in the classroom and how they are making learning happen for their own students in wonderfully engaging, fun, and worthwhile ways. I attend their presentations at the NCTE conferences. And I read the book they have written—a stunning accomplishment—for their respected colleagues around the country. And I conclude there is hope for our profession now that Terry and Michael are working in it.

Jeffrey N. Golub

ACKNOWLEDGMENTS

From Michael and Terry

First we would like to express our undying appreciation for Jim Strickland, who showed tremendous confidence in our ability to produce a worthwhile book about giving students choice in the English/language arts classroom. After seeing our presentation at the 2001 NCTE conference in Atlanta, he came up to us, held out a business card, and said, "You just presented a book. How would you like to write me a proposal?"

Next, to Gail and the staff of the Fowler Avenue location of Beef 'O' Brady's in Tampa, where we spent many Sunday afternoons occupying a booth, revising, editing, arguing, and negotiating various aspects of this text, we say, "Thank you for your patience." Often we did this without ever seeing the score of the Bucs game, and you always were there with a smile and a refill!

Most importantly, this book is for our mentor, Jeff Golub. He was first our teacher, then our colleague, and now our friend.

From Michael

This book came to be because some wonderful people believed in me and what I could bring to the table. Jeff Golub, like a well-skilled artisan, took the time to mold a wide-eyed, second-career student and guide me to actively participate in my profession. Jeff, I can never repay your contribution, but I will try to live by your example.

Independent Day School, its administration, and its staff have always given time, money, friendship, and especially patience to allow me to seek new challenges. Thank you all for helping me become a better teacher. I especially thank the Queens for being my friends and my colleagues. Working with you both and your dynamically differing personalities has always helped children and allowed me to hone my craft.

This book improved dramatically because dynamite teachers took time out of their busy schedules to give their opinions. Freda Abercrombie, a divine and trusted colleague, combed through the manuscript and asked the hard questions. Thank you so much for forcing us to answer them. To Joann

Mangru-Salmon, a wonderful friend and ESE teacher, thank you for lending your talent and expertise. I appreciate all that you did.

To Terry Bigelow, the *just-get-it-down-on-paper guy*, you have always challenged me to look beyond my classroom to a bigger world. Thank you for your generosity of spirit, kindness, hospitality, and most of all friendship.

To my parents, who have always taught me to do my best at whatever I do, I owe you everything. Thank you for instilling in me what makes me the man I am today.

Most importantly, to my wife, April, and my son, Ian, I thank God for you. You are my life. For your encouragement, early morning hugs, and constant love, I thank you. I deserve so much less, and you give me so much more.

From Terry

Again, I must acknowledge my professional father, Jeff Golub. Few people have shown greater confidence in me than him. Many times, against my will, he forced me to succeed where I didn't think I could. I am indebted to him forever.

Also to Barbara E. Brown, who is my professional mom. For the years that we cotaught classes, I was more a student than a coteacher. Many activities in this book are inspired, borrowed, or adapted from work she originated. She also was a primary reader for the original manuscript of this book. She deserves much credit for the teacher I am today.

Thanks to Randy Raber and Ann Marie Courtney, who read the manuscript specifically to make the ideas in this text useful to ESE teachers. Their insight taught us a great deal.

To my parents, who raised me to be kind, to be stubborn, to work hard, and to never settle for less than trying my best even in the face of failure. They are greatly responsible for the man I am today.

My special thanks to the staff, faculty, families, and students of Orange Grove Middle School of the Arts, my home away from home for many early mornings and late nights. I worked with arguably the best people in the state of Florida.

To Max Hutto, Anthony Perrone, and Debra Arias, who understood and supported my curious teaching habits while working on this book, your tremendous patience is appreciated.

To Michael Vokoun, the *detail guy* in this writing team; he sees the little things that I overlook and always makes my writing better—often after a hearty laugh and a "That needs a comma!" Thank you for your patience and friendship.

Finally, my greatest appreciation goes to my wife, Mary, who has an especially high tolerance for *noise and nonsense*, odd work hours, my attending conferences to learn more, and seeing her loyal, loving husband only sporadically. Without you, there is no me.

Freewill

Lyrics by Neil Peart

There are those who think that life has nothing left to chance,
A host of holy horrors to direct our aimless dance.

A planet of playthings,
We dance on the strings
Of powers we cannot perceive
"The stars aren't aligned—
Or the gods are malign"
Blame is better to give than receive.

You can choose a ready guide in some celestial voice.
If you choose not to decide, you still have made a choice.
You can choose from phantom fears and kindness that can kill;
I will choose a path that's clear—
I will choose Free Will.

There are those who think that they were dealt a losing hand,
The cards were stacked against them—they weren't born in Lotus-Land.

All preordained—
A prisoner in chains—
A victim of venomous fate.
Kicked in the face,
You can't pray for a place
In Heaven's unearthly estate.

You can choose a ready guide in some celestial voice.
If you choose not to decide, you still have made a choice.
You can choose from phantom fears and kindness that can kill;
I will choose a path that's clear—
I will choose Free Will.

Each of us—
A cell of awareness—
Imperfect and incomplete.
Genetic blends
With uncertain ends
On a fortune hunt that's far too fleet.

INTRODUCTION

How to Use This Book

English teachers teach life. English is the one class in school where students, through discussing literature and writing to express their thoughts and inform and persuade others, can see possibilities beyond their current situation. English is the one class that can help guide students as they consider the type of people they want to become. Acknowledging this tremendous responsibility drives English teachers to continually look for new and better ways to help their students perform with language. All of us have experienced days when we had the desire and the time to find out the *why* behind a particular approach when it worked.

Education has become a fast-paced, hectic world, and we need texts that can be accessed quickly and easily for a number of purposes. We hope we have made this text not only a valuable but also a useful tool for our readers. We have both been in a position in which we hadn't found an appropriate activity to address a particular problem at 7:30 in the morning when class started at 8:00! Because of this, we have taken Jim Burke's (2001) words to heart: "Some books, even such classics as James Moffett's *Teaching the Universe of Discourse* (1983), contained no index and had tables of contents that offered little guidance to the teacher on the run. Moffet's table of contents, for example, offers no guidance to help the harried teacher find his way to the many useful strategies in the book" (15).

With this in mind, we have divided this text into two distinct parts. The first, smaller part of the book is where you will find the introduction and some research into why we have chosen to give students some aspect of control over their own learning. Many of us do this because it makes sense. We know that when faced with a situation where we can make decisions for ourselves or someone else can make them for us, we will usually make our own choices. Children, like adults, crave autonomy. When we set goals and boundaries for ourselves, then we are more prone to accept the consequences and reap the benefits, rejoicing in our achievements. What better way to teach a child about life than to have him set a goal, strive to achieve it, and then delight in the accomplishment?

Teachers readily see the difference that choice can make in their students. Many of us have witnessed classrooms where students are automatons who are told what to do and when to do it day in and day out, never making decisions for themselves. These classrooms feel dark and gray no matter how bright the posters on the walls may be.

In contrast, we have witnessed classrooms where students make dozens of choices each day. These classrooms are vibrant with the murmurs of learning. We have seen this with our eyes, but when asked why it works, we've found that the research is often not readily available or on the tips of our tongues. With this text, we hope to partially serve this need.

The second part of the book is a collection of student activities, assignments, and projects that provide students with various amounts of control over their own learning. We have classroom tested these activities during our combined twenty-plus years of classroom experience.

The second part of the text has been organized into categories based on what area the activities focus on primarily. Though these sections are inherently linked by their nature, the practical part of this text is divided into the following categories to make it more accessible for various purposes: reading, vocabulary, writing, and speaking.

You will find each of the activities divided even further for your convenience. Initially, you will find the title of the activity followed by a brief explanation of what the activity entails, the problem it solved for the teacher, and how it was born. We hope that teachers will see aspects of their classrooms in this description and want to read on to see if they can use the activity in their own situations.

This is followed by an experience section titled either Michael's Experience or Terry's Experience, which contains a classroom anecdote regarding the activity. We feel that an activity comes to life when a reader can see how it played out in one of our classrooms.

The next section is titled How to Make It Happen and contains the process for the activity. If readers are rushed for time, they might skip over the anecdote and proceed right to this section. These are the ingredients of the dish and the directions for making it a meal.

The subsequent section of each of these activities is titled Adaptations. We created the Adaptations section to help readers see various aspects of each activity. If you teach a particular audience (gifted, Exceptional Student Education [ESE], younger students), want ideas on how to differentiate your instruction, want to focus on aspects of multiple intelligences, or just want to know another way to do the activity, the Adaptations section offers some new ideas and twists on the original. It is also our hope that both the activities and the adaptations inspire new twists and more adaptations that work for you in your classroom.

The ensuing section, Q & A, is where we ask and answer some common questions that we have dealt with over the years so that our readers might benefit from our experiences. Some activities lend themselves to questioning, where others are a bit more straightforward. Because of this, some activities may have a Q & A section and others may not.

Finally, each activity may end with a Further Resources section. This is where we suggest further resources such as books, websites, and articles that might be useful to someone who wants to continue to develop a particular activity.

Therefore, by looking over the setup of this book, a teacher looking for a new activity that focuses in the area of reading will be able to go directly to the reading chapter and find something useful. On the other hand, teachers who have the time and desire to find new and useful classroom approaches but also are interested in the research behind them will find the opening chapter of this book appealing.

Terry's Childhood Experience

I remember being eight years old and avoiding reading nearly as much as I avoided cooties, which disturbed my parents, especially my father, who was a voracious reader. The only thing I would read were the comics in the newspaper. My dad *cured* me by doing something brilliant. Each payday he stopped at a used bookstore on his way home from work to buy books to read over the next couple of weeks. One day he brought home a stack of comic books, everything from *Spider-Man* to *Richie Rich*, threw them on the dining room table, and simply said, "You can have those if you like. If not, let me have them, and I'll read 'em."

They stayed there for a couple of days, and then I picked one up. And I read them. All of them. In one sitting. My best friend, Gus, lived across the street, and he read them, too.

My dad started bringing home at least ten comic books each payday. Gus' dad started going to the same store and bought Gus comic books during the weeks when my dad didn't go. After a while, we began to beg to go to the bookstore so that we could choose our own. Comic books eventually gave way to Victor Appleton III's *Tom Swift* series, which I devoured in a single summer. Then I moved on to Jules Verne, and the rest is history.

My father provided choice, not only the choice to read or not but also the choice of what to read. He knew who his audience was, and he catered to me. Young boys generally love comic books, and he used them to remedy my reading resistance.

Terry's Teaching Experience

When I became a teacher, I immediately had to deal with students who were much like I was when I was a young boy. The first day of sixth grade, Brannon walked in, smiled his big toothy grin, and introduced himself with "Hi. I'm Brannon. I hate reading and writing, and I'm not going to do it." Then he proceeded to go to his seat.

As a second-year teacher, I was thrown off balance more than a little. This was the first time that a student had approached me and so proudly announced his hatred toward my love. My first reaction was to tell him why he shouldn't hate reading and writing, but even my little experience at the time had taught me that telling a student something would make as much a difference as telling my wife's cat not to scratch the furniture. I remained quiet.

I knew that Brannon might hate reading and writing now, but I thought that if I could show him that I wouldn't force it down his throat, he might find that reading and writing were at least tolerable.

This year was going to be different than my first. I had moved back to Tampa, where I had attended university and found a job at a magnet school for technology. In preplanning, when I asked about the curriculum, I was referred to "that book with the blue and white cover." "That's your curriculum," I was told. It was Nancie Atwell's *In the Middle*. I had come home.

Before school started that year, I spent time in local used bookstores, buying up as many young adult novels as I could afford. All told, I bought about 250 books for about nine hundred dollars. This would be the cornerstone of everything I did in my classroom. The reading would lead to writing, and everyone would instantly love to read and write. I wondered why every teacher didn't do this. I would become famous throughout the land as The Man Who Made Kids Love Reading and Writing.

Not quite.

It turns out that there was no magic pill or secret potion that I could have given the students to make them be drawn to my love. Just because I had a variety of books available and let them choose what they could write about, it didn't mean that they would all suddenly love to read and write and show steady improvement in these areas. I found out quickly that this reading and writing business was hard work for students and teachers alike.

What I did find easy was giving students a choice in selecting books. Everything from *Stellaluna* to *Pet Sematary* could be found on my bookshelves. Students proved to be less resistant when given free choice. Even Brannon. I had assumed that kids who didn't like to read didn't read because they weren't very good at it. Brannon proved that I was dead wrong.

Brannon immediately found Stephen King's *The Shining*. His parents approved of him reading anything if he would just read, and he jumped right in. At first I thought he had chosen the book to get a reaction from his parents and teacher and assumed he would give up on the book pretty quickly because of the difficult reading level; however, after a couple of days, I sat down to conference with Brannon:

BIGELOW: So, how's *The Shining* going?
BRANNON: Great. I've read the first 120 pages, and I love it. It's not very scary though, and it has been a little boring in parts, but I know good stuff is coming.
BIGELOW: You've read the first 120 pages? Tell me about it.

I suspected that Brannon had watched the movie and I was about to hear a summary, but Brannon proceeded to tell me, in great detail, aspects of the novel that were different from the movie, relationships with characters, clues King had given him that something weird was going to happen, what he predicted would happen, and how excited he was to find out if he was right.

I was stunned. Before thinking, I couldn't help but ask, "It sounds like you are enjoying the book. I thought you hated reading?" I wanted to kick myself. I shouldn't have reminded him of his introduction from a week ago. Now I feared that he was going to close the book, put it back on the shelf, and never crack a book open again.

I assumed wrong again.

"This is different." I sat silently, hoping he would continue. A few seconds later, he did. "This isn't a literature book. You didn't tell me to open to page 10 and read the story and then answer the questions at the end in complete sentences. You let me pick. I thought you were going to make me pick something else, and you didn't. My mom didn't. So I read it. It's good. If all stories were like this, I'd read all the time."

Wow.

This was my first lesson. When it comes to required assignments, kids like to have a choice. If this initial lesson didn't sink in, Ryan taught it to me again that same year. I had been paired with a special education teacher in a mainstreamed class that included ten Specific Learning Disorder (SLD) students and eighteen *regular* education students. My coteacher and I decided to require each student to complete each assignment without any deviation and that we would help individual students on a need basis. As far as the students knew, they were just lucky to have two teachers in their classroom instead of one.

Every day, Ryan walked in quietly, sat in the back, and avoided all contact. He rarely participated, and I think that if he could have become invisible, he would have. My coteacher and I knew he read on a third-grade level and were deeply concerned when he chose Michael Crichton's *Jurassic Park*, a book that had been turned into a blockbuster movie during the previous summer. Ryan had experienced academic failures in the past, and we felt that by allowing this choice, we would be setting him up for another one. When we asked him if he would like to make another choice, he insisted that this was the book for him, so we conceded and hoped for the best.

I'll admit that we both thought that Ryan would recap the movie, and his conferences even hinted at this.

BIGELOW: How's the book?
RYAN: Good.
BIGELOW: What makes it good?
RYAN: It's a good story.
BIGELOW: Why?
RYAN: It's cool.

And so it went.

But as the weeks went by, I noticed a certain diligence to his work. Though his reading journals showed that Ryan struggled with the basics of language expression like sentence structure and conventions, his ideas and especially his predictions were strong. This was shown best when he started comparing the book with the movie.

I was stunned!

I even called his mom, and she confirmed that Ryan had shown more persistence with this book than with any other and that he was determined to read every page even if it took him until the following summer.

Ryan finished *Jurassic Park* during the winter break, and upon his return, he chose to read *Shoeless Joe*, by W. P. Kinsella, the book the movie *Field of Dreams* was based on. He enjoyed the opportunity to compare the two formats of storytelling. Again, he plodded through it and finished before the end of the school year. The pride Ryan had in himself as a reader was enough to teach me again how important student choice can be when it comes to reading, but the biggest news was yet to come. When my coteacher retested him for his individual education plan (IEP), Ryan still showed a problem with decoding slowly, but he tested, with extended time, at grade 13+!

I know this is not typical, but it is what is possible. It could not have happened had he not been given some self-control over his own reading. Ryan was not *cured* of his reading difficulties, but when I think back to the progress we witnessed, I feel that his ability to read and comprehend had always been there. He had learned to hate reading because he had always been forced to read texts in which he had no interest. His resistance to reading had dissipated, and his testing had shown a marked improvement.

Teachers Today

If we are unsure of how important having control really is, we need only think about how many choices we make to try to get things done.

For example, summers are very precious to us as teachers. The choices can overwhelm us. Go on vacation for a week? Two? Fly or drive? Involve the kids or drop them off? Visit Aunt Mert in Oshkosh or brother Bob in Lake Zurich? Figuring out what to do during those few precious *free* days takes a plan of attack, a search engine, a map, a compass, a sense of adventure, and a really accurate set of directions.

In fact, life itself would be easier with all of these tools at our disposal, wouldn't it? Some sort of instruction manual handed to us when we went on a date? Got married? Had kids? But wait! Instead of a manual, wouldn't it be great to have giant neon signs just pop out in front of our eyes when approaching danger? Bzzz—Wrong way! Bzzz—Wrong decision! Bzzz—What are you teaching your children here?

In 2003, IBM played off this idea with a set of television spots that touted a fictional company that had created a magical invention that would solve all of its troubles. The Universal Business Adapter would be affordable, fast, and easy, and would connect "anything to everything," but in the end, IBM explained, "There is no Universal Business Adapter."

In life, if you are lucky, you are blessed with the next best equivalent to an instruction manual, neon sign, or universal adapter—a mentor, someone who guides you, consoles you, picks you up, dusts you off, and explains the choices out there. As teachers, we strive to mentor children every day. We use our time to plan lessons that engage their minds, connect to their world, and require them to think beyond the known into uncharted territory.

Also, in an age of high-stakes testing, teachers are losing the ability to choose how to help students grow in their capacity to use the English language. More and more time is being spent in classrooms preparing for achievement tests rather than learning how to achieve and truly construct meaning with language. The first chapter of this book discusses the *why* in the question Why should students have a choice in their learning? We then present a collection of classroom-tested activities that not only offer students choice but also guide all teachers to build even more choice into their everyday classroom practice.

In this book, we hope to provide numerous examples of choice that enable students to have some control over their own learning in today's classrooms.

"What Choice Do I Have?"

1

In Support of Choice

Ownership isn't something we can give to our students; however, even if we can't give it, we can create conditions that permit (or deny) students opportunities to assume responsibility for (some) decisions affecting their learning.

—Curt Dudley-Marling

Through experience, teachers learn that students become more engaged when they have some control over what they learn. As adults, we also prefer to have control over what happens to us. In the introduction we used the example of going on vacation and the choices involved. Adults don't want to be told when and where to go on vacation or what to do when we get there, what pictures to take, or which foods to sample. We want to make those choices ourselves, and the same is true with the students in our classrooms.

It seems that a concept like providing students choice in our classrooms, which is so widely accepted in our profession, would be supported by a mountain of quality, scientific research, but it isn't. Very little long-term scientific research exists in the area of student choice in the classroom. The research that is available, however, is excellent classroom-based action research, and it all supports the idea of engaging student learners by providing them power over what and how they learn.

What Is Choice, and Why Is It Important?

Student choice provides students the opportunity to have some control over their learning. Todd (1995) suggests that it is critical to give students some aspect of control over their own learning if we as teachers hope for them to become engaged in the learning process. Dewey (1990) worried that if schools simply poured learning into the heads of students and did not consider placing the child and his needs rather than content at the center of learning, students would lose their *self*, and this is a cost too great. One way to place students at the center of learning is to let them have some control over their learning. Choice is at the root of student engagement, interest, and creation of the self as a viable member of society. Nothing can be more important.

Giving control to students over their own learning has often been described as *ownership*. Donald Graves once said, "When people own a place, they look after it. When it belongs to someone else, they couldn't care less" (Calkins 1983, 23). Modern-day teachers often try to give students some ownership of their classroom by inviting them to create classroom rules or asking for student input when setting up of the room for a kid-friendly atmosphere. Extending the comforting feeling of home to the classroom is a logical step in student choice.

However, ownership also involves giving students choices within the framework of the curriculum itself. Examples of choice range from the simple to the elaborate. Students could be given a simple choice of three writing topics or given many ways that they might respond to a text. Ownership might also be as extensive and complicated as choosing a theme for a year-long research project or even choosing the methods of communication that will be used to share the results of that research (Macrorie 1988). Providing students with choice is paramount to student engagement. For example, though there may be times when students will be asked to read a novel as a class or in a small group where they are afforded limited choice, providing students with options as often as possible gives them some control and comfort in the knowledge that they have a say in their own education (Atwell 1987, 2003; Calkins 1991, 1986, 1983; Goodman 1986; Mahoney 2002; Bigelow and Vokoun 2005).

The idea of student choice and ownership in a language arts classroom stems from providing students with various amounts of control over and comfort with their learning, thereby sparking interest. This interest in their learning commands a larger investment of energy in the process, and this investment results in stronger and deeper learning on the part of the students.

An Old Concept

It is clear, even without an avalanche of support in the literature, that choice and ownership that includes a connection to students' lives has been a long-standing important ingredient to what teachers do every day. Former National Council of Teachers of English (NCTE) president Dora V. Smith (1964) supported this notion when she said in a 1944 essay:

[D]efining lists of words on the blackboard, filling in blanks in exercises, and writing themes on topics which have little relationship to what is going on at the moment in school or at home can never be suitable for development in the classroom of a wealth of opportunities for exploring the world in which children live and for stimulating them to thought and discussion concerning it. (17)

In 1918, William H. Kilpatrick formally presented his child-centered Project Method. He explained that teachers needed to put children at the center of the learning by utilizing topics of interest. By doing so, learning becomes relevant, meaningful, and purposeful. *Purposeful* learning, therefore, becomes the motivational factor for children to engage in the project.

Also, when teachers decide which pieces of *classic literature* would be best for their student population, Rosenblatt (1938) added that student choice was critical. If a teacher chooses something too alien to the adolescent child that is missing the all-too-important connection with what is happening in a child's life today, the text will in effect close the door on learning. Thus, students' ownership of aspects of their work is crucial to their success in our classrooms.

Smith's essay, Kilpatrick's methods, and Rosenblatt's ideas are powerful evidence that teachers have known the importance of choice for decades. It is important to know now that it is our choice to decide that student choice and ownership is a key to turning on every child's imagination to engage them in their own learning.

Making Good Choices

Just because teachers offer their students a choice in what happens to them in their classrooms doesn't mean they are going to make good choices. Students make decisions every day. Should I bring my materials for class? Should I bother doing my math homework? What should I wear today? One of the most important factors in this process is the teachable moment, where a student makes a poor choice but can learn from that mistake (Allington and Johnston in Roller 2001). Teachers who provide a safe classroom atmosphere for students to learn how to make choices and then learn from them ensure that their students will consciously practice this valuable life skill.

Terry's Experience

I have had many students who resisted reading and writing when they first entered my classroom. Kate never resisted; instead she seemed to thrive, until the truth was revealed. Kate was a tall, blond thirteen-year-old girl who knew how to play the *game of school* (Tovani 2000). She was successful at school, but I could tell that she was always trying to find the path of least resistance that still led to the coveted A that she craved.

When it was time to sign a revision check-off for a peer's writing, Kate knew that students needed two signed check-off sheets before the final had to be turned in, so she *played the game* and was the first to sign her name, indicating she had read and revised Robert's work when she actually hadn't. Robert, who had been looking for good advice on how to revise his work, confronted her with the signed blank revision sheet, and she declared proudly, "There were no problems!"

It's not that she couldn't do it well; it's just that she wouldn't do more than the bare minimum. Donald Graves (1983) has suggested that students will be more willing to revise and edit their own writing if given a chance to choose their topics in the first place. Kate had been given choice. She had a choice in writing topics as well as the choice of whether to do a good job for a peer when it came to revision. She chose not to do a good job, and in turn, Robert did not get the feedback he needed to improve his story properly, so he enlisted another student to help him with this step of the writing process. His going to someone else for help embarrassed Kate because she was known as the *good student* in class and did not want to lose this status. She later offered to revise the writing properly, but Robert was so irritated that he declined.

Kate made a poor decision because she didn't see where she would be held accountable. I didn't have to hold her accountable because Robert did this for me. Kate valued her peers' opinion of her as a good English student, and by making this poor choice, she injured her reputation. I saw Kate take revision seriously from this point on. She seemed to take all of her academic choices seriously after this lesson. I hope that this has carried over to her life beyond school.

Michael's Experience

Heath was a smart student that infused lyrics, poetry, writing, and singing into any and all assignments in which I would let him. He played the bass guitar, and he once had his father bring his two-hundred-pound amplifier to school for a writing presentation. If he could have sung me his vocabulary quizzes for a grade instead of doing the pencil-and-paper version, he would have.

Along with this wickedly smart and musically talented streak, Heath also rarely ever did any work that didn't interest him. If it was in a book and he was forced to read and be tested on it (vocabulary, grammar, whole-class literature), he would rather look at the clouds, write a ballad to an exciting red rock, or look up the airspeed velocity of an unladen swallow before actually accomplishing the task. However, when I offered assignments like Alternative Book Reports (Chapter 2), where the choices were open to interpretation and abundant, Heath would spend hours laboring over exactly how he would freak out his peers and his teacher. It jazzed him to be able to choose how to show what he had learned.

I was constantly in touch with Heath's parents because he often was on the verge of failing English class. Even though he had been given large amounts of choice on many of his assignments throughout his eighth-grade year, he had yet to learn that there were some parts of life that are beyond his control that still require his attention. We all have the choice not to take out the garbage, but who wants to live in it? Heath was willing to live with his grades, but his parents were not.

Though Heath was offered varying amounts of choice and control over his learning, he still needed to mature in his ability to balance what he wanted to do with what he needed to do. Adults struggle with this balance every day. It is our job as teachers to build into our curriculum options where students can learn from their mistakes.

The Hidden Curriculum

Part of the hidden curriculum in all classrooms is teaching students the skill of making good choices in the first place. Students need to know that they come to a safe place where experimentation is encouraged and both success and failure lead to learning. This can be accomplished by modeling. Teachers who show themselves to be superhuman and unable to make a mistake set their students up to believe them to be gods of English instead of the fallible humans that they are. Teachers can model making choices for their students during the writing process when deciding what to do next, during the planning process of a minilesson when deciding what to teach and why, or during the process of deciding when it is a good time to put a book down and move on to a new one. Each of these can be a life lesson for students that need to see choice in action modeled by someone that is experienced with it.

Many teachers also already know and teach students to learn in the way that is best suited for them, and some teachers would rather keep these choices hidden within the lesson or activity itself. Those teachers that are able to *let students in* on the reasoning for an activity and the options available to them allow students to better reflect on their learning and provide students with an invitation to see how they can grow as learners.

Teachers can implicitly or explicitly allow students in on the learning process. They can decide if students would benefit from knowing how a lesson is being taught or just know for themselves that the concept will be presented in many different sensory modalities, therefore reaching their entire audience (Barbe and Milone 1981). Is there value in letting students know how best to intake new information? Is it important that students realize the learning channel choices they are being offered? These choices to uncover the hidden curriculum must be up to teachers and their instructional goals.

English and language arts teachers must seek a balance between giving students control of their learning through many modalities and ensuring that they also improve in the areas of reading, writing, speaking, listening, viewing, and thinking. This equilibrium is vital to making learning important to them. Learning and school were not important to Kate, but the grade she brought home was. Free will and certain types of learning were important to Heath, but the grade he brought home was not. How do we reach all students and find each student's equilibrium? What assignments warrant choice? How much choice should we or can we allow? These are the constant balancing acts that we face as educators.

Choices in English/Language Arts Classrooms

In writing, Nancie Atwell (2003) focuses on the importance of choice in her classroom. "My students work as hard as they do on their writing, producing more than 20 publishable, and often published, pieces every year, because each writer decides what he or she will write about. Choice is the bedrock. All writers care most deeply about the projects they carve out for themselves" (17). Students work as authors, writing and learning about writing in an environment where they have complete control over their ideas. Students' own work is more important and therefore more meaningful than having every student work on the teacher's assignment, writing on the same topic in the same genre. Is it more important to engage the student in writing, or is it more important that everyone is forced to persuade the principal that there shouldn't be a dress code policy?

In reading, if all the students do is read the teacher's books and repeat the findings in those books, what have the students learned? Any student can be a parrot, but all students should at least get the chance to critically look at a piece of literature and be able to defend their opinions of what they see to be important. Paulo Freire stated in *Education for a Critical Consciousness* (1973):

> To acquire literacy is more than to psychologically and mechanically dominate reading and writing techniques. It is to dominate those techniques in terms of consciousness; to understand what one reads and to write what one understands: it is to communicate graphically. Acquiring literacy does not involve memorizing sentences, words or syllables—lifeless objects unconnected to an existential universe—but rather an attitude of creation and re-creation, a self-transformation producing a stance of intervention in one's context. (48)

Students crave to offer their own interpretations of what they have studied in class, taking advantage of opportunities to create and re-create what is new in their world, but whenever their choices of how they explain their newfound knowledge are limited, engagement diminishes.

Kohn (1998) supports this idea of choice when he says, "The best predictors [of burnout in students], it turns out, is not too much work, too little time, or too little compensation. Rather it is powerlessness—a lack of control over what one is doing" (250). By allowing students choice in and control of their learning, we open up an entire world of inquiry to them, and we must provide students a way to connect what they choose in the classroom to their own lives.

Telling students that school will benefit them *in the future* does not *sell* an English assignment or concept to most students. For many students, nothing is more important than the present moment or this weekend. What will school do for them today that will benefit them in their life today (Beers and Probst 2004; Smith and Wilhelm 2002; Wilhelm 2004a)? Students must be allowed to bring themselves to an assignment; that is, who and what they think and need must be valid in our classrooms for students to become truly engaged in their own learning.

But how do we manage that choice without becoming overwhelmed ourselves?

Management of choice is the largest control aspect that we as teachers have in any given situation. All curriculum and decisions about levels of choice come under scrutiny when deciding how much choice to infuse into a classroom. The Center on English Learning and Achievement (CELA) researchers "have seen that when students have more control over what and how they'll be learning, they tend to exert deeper levels of more extended effort in their work" (Preller 2004, 1). However, giving students choice does not mean that teachers turn over their classrooms completely; instead, teachers must manage the right amount of choice for each individual class and student (Preller 2004). Teachers will need to decide what is appropriate not only for each student but also for themselves. What level of choice will enable both their students and themselves to find comfort and deeper levels of learning while also allowing the teachers to manage the curriculum?

Some curriculum models give students complete choice with some aspects of the curriculum, and this can be a starting point of an inquiry-based curriculum. Inquiry theory in practice involves a collaborative process of students and teachers figuring out the curriculum together. Inquiry involves students asking their own questions, immersing themselves within a topic that matters to them instead of researching a required question or topic (Short 1997). This level of student choice is possible, and many teachers and groups rely upon it. The International Baccalaureate Organization (IBO) is an international education leader that has a mission that "aims to develop inquiring, knowledgeable and caring young people who help to create a better and more peaceful world through intercultural understanding and respect" (2004, 1). The basis of its teaching methods is grounded in inquiry theory, and schools that want to be considered International Baccalaureate world schools by the IBO must show their competent management of the inquiry process.

All curricula do not allow this kind of latitude in what and how to teach. Some states and districts specifically dictate what will be taught on which day. How do teachers in these circumstances infuse choice into their classrooms? They either choose to close the door and do what they think is best for their students or build choice into individual assignments that fulfill the requirements of the curriculum that they must follow.

This book offers examples of how teachers can manage their classrooms by outlining both small assignments and larger projects that all provide students with some aspect of control over their learning. Some of these examples provide students with a wealth of choice in how to create their assignment and what the final product might come to be. In other cases, students are more limited in the control they have, but aspects of choice are still given for the opportunity to place their mark on the final product, thus engaging student learners.

The Proof Is in the Pudding

Many teachers have already built choice into what students do in their classrooms every day. These teachers have already experienced what giving students control over their own learning can afford in their classrooms. In this case, we hope that this book will be reaffirming to them and will strengthen the foundation they have already built.

We also hope that the activities in this text will not be the only opportunities for choice that teachers offer students. Instead the goal of this text is to stimulate a myriad of opportunities for teachers to bend and twist existing assignments and projects to include choice and stronger ownership throughout the learning process.

Teachers have many aspects of their curriculum that they must teach or they know work for them as practitioners. We hope that after reading this book, teachers will reexamine their curricula and add one new idea that can provide their students with more opportunities to own their learning. If an additional aspect of student choice can be inserted within an assignment, the quality of the products that teachers will receive will jump exponentially. It is our hope that this book ignites the creation and improvement of assignments as well as affirms the choices that teachers already offer.

2
Choice in Reading

The things I want to know are in books; my best friend is the man who'll get me a book I ain't read.

—Abraham Lincoln

Educators would agree that reading is the most important skill to target for improvement. With good reading, anything is possible. Good readers can learn how to solve a calculus problem, learn about World War II or the Holocaust, and even figure out the atomic weight of a nitrogen atom. Reading is the entry point to understanding ourselves, others, and the world in which we live. Thus, Choice in Reading appears as the first chapter of activities in this text.

Virtually everything we do in the classroom is in response to or because of something we have read. As readers journey through this chapter, they will encounter the very beginnings of an outside reading program with the Reading Contract and move on to activities like the Brain Drawing, which can be used for an immediate response to a small piece of text in a single class period or molded to require more detailed information to test whether reading, thinking, and understanding have occurred. On a larger scale, readers will come across activities like the People Fair, which is intended to span several weeks to provide students time for a deeper understanding of another person through the completion of several assignments connected to reading a biography. Accompanying these activities are other options intended to offer students different kinds of control over their own learning, from the extremely structured Reading Memo, to the open, student-driven Mandala assignment.

These approaches to reading all offer student readers some ownership of their responses to reading. We hope you will find them useful and will make your own adaptations to these classroom-tested activities.

Reading Contract

Teachers typically struggle with ways to monitor the out-of-class reading required of their students. Leslie Boon, a former colleague at Independent

Day School, introduced Michael to a contract system that allows students to choose their books while placing a time limit on when the books, as well as any writing activities about them, will be completed.

The Reading Contract is unique for each student. Students choose their own titles, but they are only one part of a triumvirate. Their parents and teacher must agree with their choices before the contract can be accepted. But because Reading Contracts are between the students themselves, the teacher, and their parents, the students' reading and requirements become highly individualized. Dena might ask Stephen what he is reading for an idea of what to choose for her next Reading Contract, but Dena would not be able to use the defense of "But you let Stephen read it." Students need to realize and own the fact that just because they are the same age as others in the class, it doesn't mean that they are all on the same reading level. The Reading Contract is between only the individual student, her parents, and the teacher.

This powerful triangular structure promotes more familial involvement in the student's education and may finally get Tommy to read something other than fantasy or push Alison into a classic for the first time. The range of possibilities and potential for the use of the contract are endless.

Michael's Experience

As strong a structure as the Reading Contract is, if one of those involved in it drops the ball, the team doesn't score. The following three examples show how a parent, a student, and a teacher share in the responsibility of the success of the Reading Contract.

Example 1: Ann was a wonderful student who had read not only the required three novels during the summer, but all thirty-seven books that were on the suggested summer reading list! Her mother was active in the school, and she would often pop by to see what we were learning so that she could supplement Ann's learning at home to enrich what she was studying in school. If a Reading Contract was for one month and one book, Ann's mother would triple the requirements. Halfway through the year, Ann was predictably burned out. Even though she enjoyed reading, her mother was making it a chore, and Ann asked me to help. In this situation, the parent had almost completely taken over Ann's learning experience.

Example 2: Bob, on the other hand, hated to read and always did the minimum amount of reading. During free reading in school, I constantly had to make sure that Bob read (or at least looked as though he was reading) because if Bob was in a quiet room with a book, the book would likely become a pillow. When pressed about why he found reading boring, he explained: "It's dumb. I would rather skateboard."

By the time we got to the third Reading Contract, I noticed that not only had Bob always been doing the minimum amount of work, but he also had been forging his mother's signature. When I brought Bob and his mom in for a conference, his mom was exasperated. She was a lifelong reader who had been reading to Bob since he was six months old and could not understand why her son had not picked up her love of reading. It came out in the conference that instead of giving reading a chance, he had been lying to his mother, saying that reading was not a requirement of English class, pretending to read the books on the contract, and then turning in work based on summaries and reviews that he had found on the Internet. Bob was letting himself down without giving himself the chance to learn anything new and develop his ability to read.

Example 3: Then there was a time when I created the problem myself. I always thought that a teacher should give only the amount of information that a student needs to be successful, thus allowing for creative latitude on the part of the student, but I took a wrong turn, driving both the students and myself nuts!

Since students had the choice to read whatever they wanted and different reading levels were being matched, I decided that every student would read one thousand pages in the six-week contract period. Not only did I have requirements for the total number of pages to be read, but I also required a certain number of pages to be read each night. A contract addendum had to be turned in each week with both the student's and his parents' signatures that showed the student's weekly reading progress toward the prescribed and seemingly arbitrary number of pages.

This was a bit like taking the entire eighth-grade class on a field trip to the park and allowing them to play on any apparatus but asking them to prove that they had at least one thousand seconds of fun. I had, in one assignment, sucked any enjoyment out of reading for my students—the opposite of my goal as their teacher.

The Reading Contract is built, by design, to be supported by the triumvirate of the parent, the student, and the teacher. As these three examples have shown, if any one of those pillars overcompensates or undercompensates, the structure can fail.

How to Make It Happen

1. Teachers need to decide what their reading program will require of them, their students, and the parents. These requirements need to be built into the Reading Contract itself. Michael's basic Reading Contract includes blanks for the title, the author, and the number of pages for the books being read (he allows for spaces for up to four books) as well as the due date of the contract, a parent signature, and a student signature. The style of the contract is open to the teacher's prerogative, but the more official it looks, with blue ribbons or seals of approval, the better.

2. Teachers need to set some realistic time frames and expectations for student reading. The larger the time frame, the more unmanageable the contract and the subsequent assignments. Also, some students need to be challenged to read other genres, higher reading levels, or more thought-provoking material. In some cases teachers will have a student like Bob and will be thrilled that he is reading at all. In other cases they will want to challenge students who already love reading to branch out from their comfort zones.

3. Teachers should be sure to keep a copy of each contract as a record of what students have accomplished as well as a reminder of what they may need to try next time. Also, signatures are easy to fake, and having the contract there to help with parent conferences is important.

4. The *assignment* that the students must do to complete their contract must also be made clear ahead of time. Many of the ideas that are detailed later in this chapter can be used as Reading Contract assignments that have the students prove their new understandings of themselves and the world around them.

One of the beauties of Reading Contracts is that even though students have an open invitation to choose their books, they must also communicate with their families and their teacher to negotiate a contract that will satisfy all parties. This added element of a check-and-balance system prevents students from choosing books that will not challenge them or that may cause them great difficulty while also allowing parents to participate in the education of their children. Though the triangular structure is a strong one, the major strength of the Reading Contract lies in the ability to choose.

Adaptations

- Jeff Wilhelm (2003), noted reading authority, suggested that there is value in having two or three students read the same novel at the same time. For whatever reason, Michael had never offered small groups of students the opportunity to read the same book at the same time, and when he did he was pleasantly surprised at the depth of students' responses and conversations about their books and the impressiveness of the assignments that they produced. The added element of being able to debrief and appreciate the book (or tear it apart) together took on deeper meaning and provided a larger connection for those students who took advantage of this opportunity.

- The adaptation of having students read a book with another student cannot be forced, though. At first Michael made the mistake of requiring students to at least pair up with one other student to read a book together. The students had full control of whom to pair up with, but some collaborations still ended in disaster. In one instance, a reading pair began as friends, but because of a series of misunderstandings, miscommunications, and conflicting schedules outside of school, the two students, and even their parents, no longer speak to each other. Now Michael offers this opportunity to read together often and allows students two options: reading a book with others or reading individually. Some find reading together very rewarding, some try it and never do it again, and some are content to read alone and be in charge of their own responsibilities.

- Differentiated Instruction: The number of books required and the amount of time given for the contract are the easiest changes to make. If the students have the will and drive to sink their minds into one of those *big books*, but their reading speed is slower than most, larger books can be broken into smaller chunks to be read over many Reading Contracts. If students make a breakthrough and find a book that they enjoy reading, but it takes them many contracts to complete it, teachers should allow this differentiation to help nurture a love of reading.

- If parents are unavailable to be involved with a child's education, teachers might utilize a different authority figure as part of the Reading Contract triumvirate, such as a guidance counselor or a caseworker, especially when working with an ESE student.

Q & A

What is the average number of books that students sign up for?

Michael's contracts are usually for a minimum of one or two books. It depends on the length of the contract and the level of the student. When working with any student, but especially ESE students, teachers should ask themselves whether the time allotted in the contract is enough for the student to grasp the amount of material successfully. The objective will be different for each student.

What is the average length of a Reading Contract?

Michael's experience has been that the shorter the contract period, the better. To allow for varying reader speeds, he has most frequently used a one-month contract.

Can Reading Contracts work with 150 students?

They sure can. This is a totally individualized reading program, and having a few systems in place will make it run smoothly. A reading log, which students keep up-to-date with each book read, helps the teacher know which book a student is working on at any given time. Reader response is another way to require students to show that they are reading, so if time is available for the teacher to respond to all of them, response formats might work. In the end, the Reading Contract is a wonderful paper trail for a teacher who needs to document student progression in reading.

How will each student prove that he has read his book?

Having the end in mind is important. This chapter describes several reading activities that can be options for this part of the students' learning process. Work that can be required of students can vary from differing types of reflections at regular intervals to large-scale reports. The choice is up to the teacher as to how she wants to customize the kinds and amount of proof that she expects from her students.

Do Reading Contracts work for ESE/ELL students?

They sure can. ESE and ELL (English language learner) students may need to have more guidance and possibly a range of books to choose from, but the concept is still the same. Students are more apt to read books that they have had a hand in choosing.

Reading Memo

Language arts and English teachers subscribe to the belief that their students must read outside of class to improve their ability to read. Some teachers require standing assignments of outside reading each school night or a specified time spent reading each week. One of the challenges this approach poses, besides holding the attention of resistant readers, is making students accountable and providing them with a way to get credit for this reading. Teachers have tried many methods to provide students with an unobtrusive, fair, and engaging way to respond to their reading but often have been resigned to using something less satisfying. Some methods take a tremendous amount of time, thus interfering with students' reading. Some do not engage readers. Some are fantastic, unique ways for students to respond but might not be particularly appropriate for a specific outside reading or class of students.

These concerns led Barbara E. Brown, a teacher in Tampa, Florida, to design a reading memo, based on the basic business memo, which provides students with a reasonable, straightforward, and brief way to respond to their independent reading. The original format included a typical memo heading, a brief summary, a place for questions from the reader, and a personal response. This layout has been adapted to consider current research and to address specific reading response skills.

Terry's Experience

When the year began, a small, quiet girl named Stacey came into my class and immediately found a seat in the back where she could hide behind her glasses, freckles, and other students. She smiled when spoken to and sometimes contributed in class when she seemed to feel especially confident. She ultimately retaught me just how valuable Reading Memos and personal ownership in choosing books can be to students.

Six weeks into the year, I had to miss a Friday and left plans for the substitute: "My students want time to read. Let them read. Don't interfere with this, and make sure to redirect students who get *distracted* back to their reading. This way they won't disturb each other."

I was astounded when I found an email from Stacey's mom saying that her daughter had come home disappointed because the substitute had let kids *run wild*, and that she hadn't been able to read. Up until that point I had not been able to get a clear picture of Stacey's outside reading habits, but this showed me her great attitude toward reading. Stacey's mom thanked me for turning Stacey back into a reader after competitive elementary reading programs had turned her off from reading. Since entering middle school, Stacey did not really read beyond minimum requirements in sixth or seventh grade. Her mother said that Stacey had been talking about books and completing Reading Memos for my class without resistance because "they [made] sense," and "[didn't] waste her time."

I cannot take credit for turning Stacey back into a reader. All I did was give her a choice of what she read and a subtle way to respond. Sometimes simple success is right beneath our noses, and we don't even realize it.

How to Make It Happen

The Reading Memo's current format fits on the front and back of one sheet of paper. Memos are created and stored in each student's one-subject notebook throughout the year and become a record of each student's reading, offering insight into his thoughts as the year progresses.

It would be ideal to be able to conference with each individual student for even a brief period of time each week about her reading, but this is nearly impossible in a modern school setting in which teachers have at least five or six forty-five-minute periods each day and often see more than 140 students. Instead, the memo allows teachers to write questions and short comments to readers and carry on brief but meaningful conversations with them about their reading; they can look for answers in successive memos.

1. To introduce students to the memo format, it is critical that teachers model the process. Terry has seen hundreds of student-inspired variations of the memo directions over the years. One way to prevent many of these less responsive versions is to read a short story in class and take students through the expectations for each section of the memo.

2. Part I, the heading, is done in a business memo format, but the choice of audience means that the memo can be written for specific purposes. For example, students will write the memo differently if they are writing to their teacher, a friend, or a parent. When students change the audience the memo addresses, the perspective of the writing changes. This is an opportunity for a teacher to show students how audience can impact their voice in writing. For many students, especially ESE students, when teachers allow them to write in the voice with which they are most comfortable, the students become more willing to contribute.

3. The "From" section offers the same kinds of options for the memo because it can be written from the perspective of the reader, a character in the book, or even a character in another book. For example, students could write as Ponyboy in *The Outsiders* responding to *Night*, by Elie Wiesel. This would certainly make students stretch themselves; they'd need to enact one character dealing with one kind of oppression and determine how that character might respond to a story about another kind of oppression. Students can also just be themselves and talk to their teacher about their insights.

4. When introducing the heading, teachers should wait to offer any variations to the heading format until students have done a few memos on their own. When modeling the first memo with a short story, teachers should have all students use the same format.

5. Part II contains a brief summary of the reading for the week. This summary should fill only the rest of the front of the paper *except* for the last five or six lines. This requires students to carefully choose which events to include in their summary. It forces them to be concise and decide what belongs here and what does not. This is an exercise in thinking about what is important enough to include in the short space provided as well as a reading comprehension practice for main idea.

6. Part III takes up the last five or six lines of the front side of the memo and contains questions generated by the reader. This is the place where students record a few of their *I wonder* thoughts from the reading. They may list questions they want to ask the author or questions for characters in the story or questions to the teacher or themselves as readers. This provides students a place to become aware of and document the questions that come to mind while they read. A student might ask Johnny in *The Outsiders*: "Why did you risk your life to go into the burning church to save the children?" This can be seen in Figure 2–1.

7. When the first three parts of the memo are complete, students should flip their paper over and divide the back of the page in half with a horizontal line. This provides them with two equal halves of the paper to complete the final two sections of the memo.

8. Part IV of the memo is the visualization section. This section asks students to draw a scene or two from their reading that struck them because they were important to the story, they elicited an emotional response, or they reminded them of events in their life and world. Creating a drawing of what they perceive as the most important or memorable events in a section of reading is a powerful learning opportunity for students. It provides an opportunity for the ESE/ELL student to communicate his ideas about what he has read as well. In his research on engaged reading, Jeff Wilhelm (2004b) found that being able to "create images, story worlds, and mental models while one reads is an essential element of reading comprehension, engagement, and reflection" (9). Of course, they are not judged on their artistic ability but rather on the thought and time spent to accurately represent the scene(s). Stick people are acceptable!

new notebook?

I Heading:
To: Mr. Bigelow
From: Allison
Re "The secret Life of Bees" p. 27-86 97-A
40/40

II Summary:

On Lily's fourteenth birthday, T-Ray told Lily that her mother planned on leaving him and Lily to start anew life. T-Ray said that Lily's mother didn't love her and wanted nothing to do with her. Lily, not being able to live with a man who could say such a thing, ran away. She planned on going to Tribron, South Carolina, when her mother had been before. [margin: the day she died before]

Lily helped excape Rosealeen from jail/the hospital, and they were on their way to Tribron. Lily and Rosealeen walk for forever before a kind black man offered to drop them off three mile before Tribron. The man dropped the two of them off and they walked to a near by store.

It was a Sunday, so customers were not allowe to buy store items, but they were allowed to buy food from the side restraunt. Lily was waiting for her food and saw a hunny jar that had a picture of a black virgin mary, just like the one that had belonged to her mother. Lily asked the person that worked there who made the hunny. He said a lady named August, and gave her directions to August's house.

III Question:

- Why is August's house bright pink?
- Why does May sing "Oh, Susanna"?

FIGURE 2–1a. *Allison's Memo (front side)*

9. Students use the second half of the back page for their explanation and response (Part V). They explain what they have drawn and give a detailed and well-thought-out reason for choosing this particular scene over all other possible choices. The connections they make to their own lives are what draw them into interacting with a text. "Literature invites the reader to observe his own responses, to see himself as if in a photograph, some aspect of his emotional or intellectual self frozen

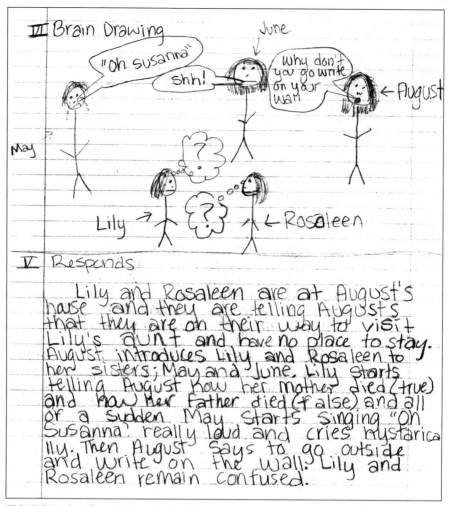

FIGURE 2–1b. *Allison's Memo (back side)*

and awaiting inspection; thus it rewards the reader with sharpened understanding of himself" (Probst 1988, 23).

Utilizing this memo approach to reader response holds students account-able for their outside reading and is beneficial for both the students and the teacher. Students know that the reading is their priority. They know this because teacher *actions* back it up. The memo should not take more than fifteen or twenty minutes to complete. The bulk of time should be spent on reading, and students' *payment* in the form of points is relatively easy to obtain. Students decide what and how to include information under the headings of the memo chosen by their teacher. Teachers benefit because they have a manageable way for their students to respond to their reading and can stay on top of the texts and thoughts their students are experiencing.

Adaptations

- Teachers can change the audience to whom the memo is addressed— for example, a friend, a parent, another teacher, a character from the book, or even a character from another book.
- The student could take on the persona of a character in the book or another book and write the memo from that character's perspective.
- Teachers also have the prerogative to change Parts II–V to suit their needs. All of the parts of the memo can be adapted and adjusted to serve the needs of any age level or curriculum. If teachers are interested in students being aware of difficult vocabulary in their reading, they could make one of these a "My Words" section. Students could be required to list a particular number of words from the week's reading and record the page, paragraph, or sentence in which each word was used and what that word means. The choices for these sections of the memo are limitless.
- Differentiated Instruction: Students can complete modified Reading Memos without losing the same experience as other students. The teacher will need to decide what portions of the memo are most important to gear the memo for that audience.
- Interdisciplinary Instruction: This is an activity that can be used in any classroom, and sharing this activity with all teachers in every discipline within the school can allow for consistency when dealing with the requirements of reading for information and meaning.
- If working with students that are easily distractible, teachers should try to isolate one reading skill at a time. Sequencing can be the first skill mastered, and then the student might move on to finding the main idea. For ESE teachers, Reading Memo goals could coincide with an individual education plan's comprehension goal.

Q & A

What do I do if students refuse to create the memos in response to their reading?

Depending on the individual student, teachers can decide if the student would be willing to do any response at all. If so, they may ask the student to adapt the sections of the memo to suit his needs as a reader. If students have input into how their memo will be constructed, they may be more willing to create a response to their reading. Teachers might sit down with a reluctant student and customize the memo to fit the student. They may negotiate a summary requirement and then let students choose what to write about in two of the remaining three sections. Whatever is decided, it is important to get all students engaged in their outside reading, and the flexibility of the memo allows just that.

Is the memo meant to monitor student reading on a weekly basis or longer?

Memos can be adapted for various uses. They are a short, easy way for students to respond to their reading and for teachers to conduct an efficient, ongoing conversation with students about their reading. They can be used weekly, biweekly, or after reading an entire text.

How many memos should be done for one book, or does this vary depending on the student?

Terry has veered away from requiring students to read any particular number of pages each week. When students are required to read a certain number of pages, they lean toward easier books. Terry has found that expecting students to read for a particular amount of time each week has been the most effective approach. This means that a student who reads Dean Koontz and a student who reads a *Fear Street* book will both be able to find success with the assignment.

How labor-intensive is responding to 140 students if this is done on a weekly basis? Are there ways to cut down on the paper load?

Initially, Reading Memos can be labor-intensive because teachers need to make sure students understand what is expected in each area of the assignment. Are they filling in the heading correctly? Are the questions they are asking going deep enough? Once students have completed several memos, communicating with them about their reading becomes more enjoyable and feels less like work.

Further Resource

Rosenblatt, Louise M. 1978. *The Reader, the Text and the Poem: The Transactional Theory of the Literary Work.* Carbondale, IL: University of Illinois Press.

Brain Drawing

Like many teachers, Terry is constantly on the lookout for new ways for his students to respond to texts, responses that allow for certain types of social interaction; constructive, deep exploration of meaning; and students' active involvement. Several years ago, Terry saw a proposed, but never actually used, version of the California Writing Test (Blau 2001) that was full of great elements for classroom teachers. One of these elements was called the Open Mind. It asked students to portray how a particular character might be feeling or what he or she might be thinking at a particular point in the story. This portrayal was to be done by filling in an outline of a human head with symbols, words, images, phrases, or a combination of these.

Terry thought of a number of variations that were possible for particular situations. Years later, when faced with a group of students who were struggling to see stories from the characters' perspectives, Terry remembered the Open Mind activity. He was looking for a way for students to think about characters, to walk in their shoes and slip into their skins, and before Terry could track down the original version of the Open Mind activity, the current version of the Brain Drawing was born.

The Brain Drawing gives students a chance to think abstractly and specifically focus on a character in a text. Students can choose the symbols to use and be as creative as they like. Another positive quality of the Brain Drawing is that it can be used as an in-class activity to spark discussion, as a *test* to compare two characters, or as a homework assignment that follows specific directions and a rubric. The Brain Drawing is a simple activity, but the power of the visualization makes this a strong tool for both the teacher and the students.

Terry's Experience

Alana rarely participated in discussions about texts read in or for class. Some teachers might think she was shy, but in the hallways before, between, and after classes she was outgoing, energetic, and enthusiastic. She just didn't seem to want to share her thoughts in class.

"Hey, Alana, come here," I said one day before class began. "We're going to read a cool story today in class, and I was hoping that I could count on you to join in the discussion. All I want to ask is that you share one thing during the discussion. When I see you raise your hand, I'll know that you are ready to add something to the conversation."

"I dunno," she said. She licked her lips and looked over her shoulder. "The stories we read in class are usually good and everything, but I just don't have much to say about them." And she walked away.

I was frustrated. Usually if I asked students point-blank like this, they would agree to let me involve them in the discussion. I felt this was more fair than calling on students when they weren't ready, a practice I felt set them up to look bad in front of their peers and led to their being more resistant to participating in class in the future.

Alana refused to give me an opening to get her involved. I thought that if I could just get her to become involved in a class discussion once, she might be hooked for the rest of the year. I could tell from her writing that she had a great deal to offer other students and her teacher, so I was determined to reach her.

Around the same time, I also noticed that students were not understanding characters' motivations in the stories we read. I tried some role-playing games, but none allowed students to see the perspective of the characters, to understand how good readers could analyze decisions characters made by getting into a character's head, even if the reader would not choose the same action.

Then I decided to try the Brain Drawing activity, and I prepared several versions to try (see the Adaptations section for some of these).

I found an outline drawing of a human head on the Internet, enlarged it to fill an 8½-by-11-inch piece of paper, and made copies for class. Throughout the day I tried different versions of the activity. Many of them worked well, but I was still looking for the piece of the puzzle that was missing.

Alana had the missing piece.

I had had some real success with students reading "The Fan Club," by Rona Maynard, a story about a ninth-grade girl named Laura and her peers who mistreat her. Its surprise ending always elicits gasps and "No ways" from students.

Alana walked into her seventh-period class, and I figured that she would do her usual fantastic job on the activity but participate as little as possible. At the end of the story, I passed out copies of the blank head outline, and I asked students to use only symbols (no words) to indicate what Laura was thinking and feeling at the point in the story where she thought she was the target of some malicious peers. After a few questions, students got down to business and worked diligently. Eventually, I asked students to show their Brain Drawings to at least one other student and explain what they had done. Alana worked with Jacob, who sat right next to her. I didn't think anything of their discussion until I gave the students a chance to share the best ideas they'd had.

Jacob's hand shot up, and I called on him.

"Alana had the coolest idea! She drew stuff inside the head, like you said, Mr. B., but then she also drew stuff *outside* the head. She showed how Laura felt on the inside but also how she wanted people to view her by her drawing on the outside of the head! Alana, you tell them!"

"Ummm," she hesitated.

"Come on!" Jake pleaded.

Everyone waited as her eyes shifted back and forth across the class.

"Well, for example, inside I drew a cloud with lightning coming out of it to show how mad she is with herself for going along with the Fan Club, but on the outside I drew an ice cube to show how cool she is trying to be in front of the cool kids."

"Yeah!" some kids exclaimed.

Hands shot up all over the room. Kids immediately started sharing ideas they had for Alana's version of the Brain Drawing. There was even discussion of other stories we had read and how particular characters seemed to show the world one thing when they were feeling something different inside. During this discussion using Alana's idea, other students began adding symbols and ideas to the outside of their Brain Drawings before turning them in (see Figure 2–2).

The rest is history. I now use several versions of this activity, depending on the situation and what I am hoping to accomplish, but I am especially fond of Alana's version because it sparked a shy, intelligent young lady to begin participating in class, if only from time to time. Alana never magically became the leader of our class discussions, but she slowly began to feel confident enough to offer ideas when she had them. Her success, in the eyes of her peers, made this happen. Alana found a great way to show what was happening inside a character's head as well as what she was trying to show the story world on the outside and how these might be different.

Had Jacob not pushed her to share this in class, I would have missed an opportunity to include Alana in the discussion, and our discussion of the story might not have been nearly as rich that day. And I might never have had the strong idea to graphically show not only what is happening within a character's mind but also how that differs from what the character shows to the world.

How to Make It Happen

1. The first step is to find or create an outline drawing of a head or a brain. Most teachers have at least one student who is a good artist and

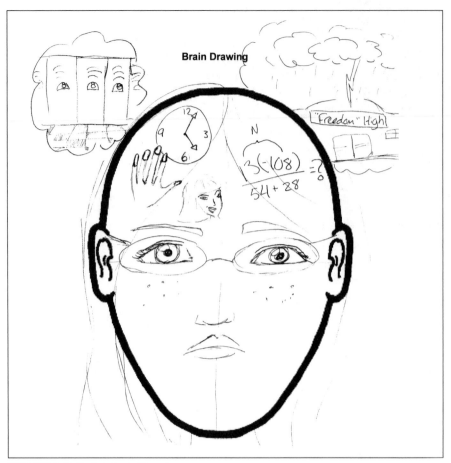

FIGURE 2–2. *Emily's Brain Drawing*

can deliver what is needed. Teachers could even allow the artist to sign his or her name in the corner so that every student who uses the sheet will know who created the artwork!

2. The next step is to decide at what point to have students stop reading and record their reactions. Terry suggests giving students the story only up to the point of discussion and keeping the rest of the story on a separate handout to be given out later. This prevents curious students from reading ahead to discover secrets that characters might reveal later in the story. This also whets their appetite for the remainder of the tale.

3. Students then complete a Brain Drawing. Teachers might give students only ten minutes to do this in class. If so, the drawings will likely not

be in color, nor will they be as complete as they could be, given more time, but they will be sufficient to inspire a quality discussion.

4. Teachers must make sure that students have an audience for their work. Continuing with the example of the in-class Brain Drawing, teachers need to ask students to show their work to at least two other students who sit near them and explain why they made the particular decisions they made. Terry also asks that the person who views the work to sign his or her name on the back of the paper. This gives an *official* feel to this process as well as ensuring that all students will have an audience for their work. It might even inspire some to share out loud in class (Golub 1994).

5. After the students share with their neighbors, the teacher should lead students through a discussion of the best ideas they saw. Often, students disagree about what a character is feeling and must go back to the text to support their ideas. This type of discussion rarely runs out of steam, so the teacher will have to decide when and how to stop this process.

The Brain Drawing offers teachers a way to have students deeply explore characters from a text and gives students a chance to show their creativity through the symbols they choose to represent the elements that they feel make up a character's personality. This opportunity for students to be creative and bring themselves to the text is the factor that makes this activity appealing to students of all ages.

Adaptations

- Teachers could allow students to compare two characters by either copying the head outlines back-to-back or asking students to divide one head in half, using a line that indicates the characters' relationship. If the characters are enemies, the line might be jagged to indicate a rocky relationship. If they are friends, a light, thin, or dashed line might be appropriate to indicate a more amicable connection. One piece of paper with two heads on it might work; a Venn diagram made with two heads might visually depict the relationship even better.
- Teachers may use the inside–outside idea from the anecdote about Alana. If there is a situation in which a character might be feeling one way on the inside and showing the world another side, this would be a chance to allow students to explore the dichotomy by drawing inside and outside of the head outline.
- Differentiated Instruction: Teachers can use the Brain Drawing as an

assessment by providing the head outline after reading any text. The students would then explain in writing or discussion the symbols they used and why they were appropriate for this particular character.

- Students could use various symbols to create an abstract face in which each symbol represents a part of the face: the eyes, the lips, the nose, the eyebrows, and the hair. The symbols should be appropriate, and the expression on the face could be indicative of how the character is feeling.
- Students can use the limited space inside the head outline to write a character response to a text from the point of view of the character. This teaches conciseness as well as point of view.
- Teachers could introduce the use of color and discuss different colors' connotations and symbolism. For example, red can symbolize lust, blood, hate, and love while green can symbolize envy, greed, or naïveté. After teachers have had this introduction, students could then draw their Brain Drawing symbols with these colors in mind, thus adding another layer to the meaning of the assignment. Students would then indicate in writing what each of the colors represents while also explaining their symbols.
- Interdisciplinary Instruction: Students could use the Brain Drawing to explain what they believe anyone in history was thinking at any one time. This especially lends itself strongly to those units that the English and social studies classes are already studying together or as a bridge if those disciplines aren't connected yet.

Q & A

Why is drawing this information better than writing it out or just saying it out loud in a discussion format?

The Brain Drawing gives students a chance to think about what they have read from a particular character's perspective. Using symbols instead of words makes them think that much more deeply. They must think about not only how the character might feel about a particular situation but also how to symbolize these feelings metaphorically. This method is especially helpful to ESE students because it allows them to express themselves in a manner that is not so concrete. This activity takes only a small step away from the concrete and allows them to take a walk in the world of abstract thought without feeling overwhelmed.

Will any time be needed to teach students to use pictures to show information symbolically?

Terry has found that eighth graders of varying language arts abilities need little prompting to be able to do this activity. If possible, teachers should have an overhead prepared of the head outline and use a recently assigned story to model what students need to do. Two or three examples of characters should be enough to get students rolling. Younger, ELL, or exceptional education students may need more modeling than others.

What are common symbols that are used, and what do they symbolize?

The symbols are highly individual, but teachers might provide general examples, as discussed in the answer to the previous question. However, the unique symbols that students create are one of the best inspirations for class discussion. If a teacher were to say, "If a character is angry, you might draw a cloud," the danger is that then all students will draw a cloud as one of their symbols. Terry believes the fewer examples teachers give to students, the greater chance students will develop their own imagination and creativity.

Is the drawing of the symbols just for discussion in class, or is the write-up and explanation from the students a required step in the process?

The Brain Drawing can be used to spark a class discussion, as an element of the Reading Memo, as a homework assignment, or as a test. Teachers can decide how to incorporate the Brain Drawing into the writing and discussion that take place about texts in their classrooms.

Further Resources

Blau, Sheridan. 2001. "Politics and the English Language Arts." In *The Fate of Progressive Language Policies and Practices*, edited by C. Dudley-Marling and C. Edelsky, 183–208. Urbana, IL: NCTE.

Golub, Jeffrey N. 2000. *Making Learning Happen: Strategies for an Interactive Classroom*. Portsmouth, NH: Heinemann.

Wilhelm, Jeff. 2004. *Reading IS Seeing: Learning to Visualize Scenes, Characters, Ideas, and Text Worlds to Improve Comprehension and Reflective Reading*. New York: Scholastic.

Mandala

> *The Mandala is a circular form that carries within it the complete essence or nature of whatever it is you are exploring.* —Barbara E. Brown

Many teachers struggle to find ways for students to respond personally to a text. They want an assignment that allows students to think metaphorically about their reading and to respond in a unique way. They want an assignment that inspires even reluctant readers to show their thoughts and emotions in response to a text as well as to juxtapose themselves and their lives with characters and events.

The Mandala allows for each of these types of responses. Adapted from the classroom work of Barbara E. Brown, the Mandala requires metaphorical thinking about events or characters in a text as well as in the reader's life; it requires an artistic response and forces readers to examine themselves closely using the lens of the text.

Terry's Experience

Many students have challenged me over the years, but few have challenged me to the point of wanting to quit on them. One student, Danny, though a brilliant, energetic young man, was often unable to focus his enthusiasm appropriately. I spent the first half of the school year working harder than he did to prevent him from failing the eighth grade. When major assignments were due, I would sometimes call his house for several nights to remind him and his parents how important it was that he spend a few minutes getting it done. He made me reexamine whether what I asked students to do was really worthwhile. I thought to myself, "If this bright student won't do the work, obviously he doesn't find it worth doing." At midyear, I was ready to give up on Danny, telling myself, "You can't save them all." Looking back, I realize this was a cop-out on my part.

After the winter break, we were to read *The Outsiders*, a requirement at the time in my district, after which students would choose from several options for responding to this text. I knew Danny would avoid any kind of response, so during my winter break I did not even consider him when I thought about options that students might enjoy and find worthwhile.

I decided that the Mandala would be the type of response I would require. It had everything I wanted. It allows students to examine characters in the text and compare these characters with themselves, to think metaphorically and to play with language, to create an artistic response, and to write a concise, all-encompassing *essence statement*. It would certainly require them to think deeply about what they had read.

I explained the way students would be expected to respond before we read Hinton's novel. Some students had questions, but generally there was a fervent buzz in the air. As we read the novel, Danny's interest seemed to wax and wane, depending on how his day had gone when he arrived in third period. The surprise came when I built in two class periods so students might begin working on their Mandalas, asking questions and working on ideas together. I was careful not to tread on the discussions when I was not needed.

The biggest surprise was Danny. For the first time in my memory, he was focused and engaged for two days in a row. He worked diligently on the Mandala predrawing chart and was never distracted by students around him. I still wondered if I would see a final product. When the due date arrived, I was stunned to see that Danny had come to class with his assignment. He was usually fine with doing assignments in class if he was in the mood, but I could not recall him ever turning in an assignment on time that required time spent outside of class, at least not without constant prodding. Danny's Mandala finally showed what he was capable of doing when he cared. I had found the right opportunity at the right time for my most resistant student.

I would love to say that this assignment turned Danny around and that he went on to become the valedictorian of his high school class. He did, however, begin to mature, and he graduated from high school and entered college to study business. This was victory enough. The Mandala had provided him with an outlet that fit him. After he did this assignment and showed me what he could do, I could always go back to the Mandala and say, "But Danny, I've seen what you can do. Do it again!"

How to Make It Happen

The Mandala offers students a chance to think deeply about themselves and the text. I find it easy to explain, and students find the assignment engaging.

1. Teachers must discuss the definition of a Mandala with their students. Barbara E. Brown defined the Mandala as "a circular form that carries within it the complete essence or nature of whatever it is you are exploring." Examples of past student work might stunt creativity. Instead, teachers could hand out to each student a blank 8½-by-11-inch piece of paper with a circle on it and explain that what he creates on this page will represent both himself and a character with which he feels a personal connection. That should open the doors for creativity rather than close them.

2. Next, teachers can discuss the symbolism of circles. This can be a light discussion or a homework assignment. What are the qualities of a circle? What does a circle symbolize? What properties does it possess? What in life acts as a circle? Dynamic discussions could happen early in this process, but they also could take place after the kids have

finished their Mandalas. It is important that teachers allow each class to determine when this discussion will take place.

3. A discussion about the rubric is also a must. With this assignment, it is critical that students know what the *target* is so that they can hit it, and the rubric spells out the dimensions of a complete assignment. Terry includes the following categories for a basic Mandala rubric: color, neatness, explanation of symbols, essence statement, and how well students define the two items being compared.

4. Next, students can fill out the predrawing chart (Figure 2–3), which asks students to compare themselves with a character in the text with words first so that they can eventually transfer their ideas from the written word to symbolic drawings. Teachers should direct students to think of their personality when filling out the chart. For example, under the category of color, students should not write in their favorite color, but instead a color that is reflective of their personality. A person who has a short temper or is easily embarrassed might choose a color that is indicative of this, such as red, even though her favorite color may be blue. Next, the student must provide an adjective to describe that color that also fits her personality. In this case, *burning red* might be a good choice.

5. Once the predrawing chart has been completed both for the student and for the character that he has chosen, the next step requires that the student choose a number of these ideas and create drawings or symbols from the words he chose for himself and the character. These should be drawn and colored according to the requirements spelled out in the rubric.

6. Next, students begin to plan their Mandala. Students must decide how their Mandala will be divided to show the similarities and differences between themselves and the character. If the two items being compared are similar, then the line that divides them could indicate this by being soft and wavy. If the comparison is in stark contrast, then the line might be jagged or thick and bold. If the characters are like oil and water, students might make the division line look like barbed wire. Teachers should encourage students to be creative when making these decisions.

7. Then the students transfer the drawings, symbols, and lines to their final Mandala. Teachers should provide students with a perfect circle on a regular sheet of copy paper. The circle should fill the page but leave enough room for students to write the essence statement around the outside of the circle. See Liz's example in Figure 2–4.

Two-Person Mandala

Name: Monty   Kiesha

	Character:		Character:	
	Self	**Adjective**	**Other**	**Adjective**
Career	Physcologist	He is understanding he thinks in different ways	School teacher	She is understanding to a certain point
Plant or Animal	Good a dragon	I think monty is strong and tough on the inside.	a Vine	because I think she leans alot from her experience and teaching years
Color	Yellow	I think its a really innocent color.	Baby blue	Its strong like the ocean, but gentle to
Musical Instrument	Cello ?	I think its big and sweet	Harp	Its cords are long and drawn out, feels like never ending
Hobby	writing stories	imagintive, I think he could express himself well	Painting	Its colorful, I think Kiesha is a colorful person
Most Meaningful Possession	toy action doll	he thinks it protects him.	Her diary	She likes to express her self to things she know won't tell
Element (Air, Earth, Water, Fire)	Earth	he is a great support	Air	She's always there but sometimes goes unnoticed

Adapted from Barbara E. Brown

FIGURE 2–3. *Two-Person Mandala Predrawing Chart*

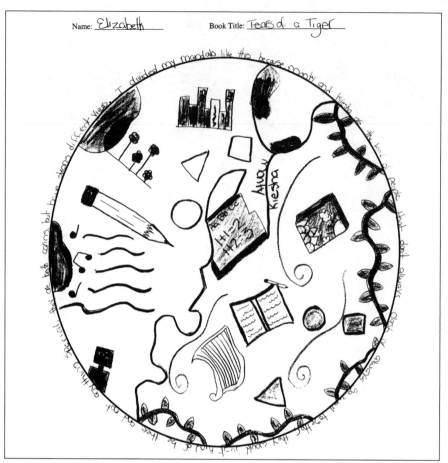

FIGURE 2–4. *Elizabeth's Mandala Drawing*

8. Finally, students should draft and revise a statement that incorporates ideas and thoughts about the relationship between themselves and the character. This statement will encircle the Mandala. It is the tie that binds their relationship as well as the symbol of the circular nature of the assignment.

The Mandala allows students to delve deeply into their personal connection with a character from a text. Since readers form some kind of bond with characters while reading, this gives students an opportunity to express this relationship and represent it visually.

Choice is built into this assignment in several ways. One of the ways that students have ownership is through their choice of character. The

Mandala provides a chance to explore profoundly their identification with any character. In a teacher-driven assignment, the teacher might not think that a student would want to use a secondary character from the book because the teacher doesn't share that student's or character's experience. Allowing the choice extends the invitation for students to connect to any one of the characters.

Another way that ownership is provided is through allowing students to choose the symbols and graphics they feel best represent their ideas. Students make these decisions. Teachers may suggest some ideas, but ultimately the students decide what is important to them and what fits best. Students have control over the final product.

Adaptations

- Students can compare two characters from the same book (protagonist and antagonist) or even characters from different books. This forces students to recall similarities and differences between the characters.
- Students can use the Mandala to compare one text with another.
- Teachers may use the Mandala to compare themes such as love and hate or peace and war.
- The predrawing chart could be changed to reflect ideas on which the teacher wants students to focus.
- Differentiated Instruction: Color and its symbolism could become a requirement or offered as extra credit for those students that can go beyond the drawing of the symbol and incorporate the deeper meanings of color as well.
- Differentiated Instruction: Students can create a practice Mandala in class in which they compare themselves with another student so that they have a clear idea of what they are required to do when they have to do so for themselves and a character within a book. Teachers should have the students present their ideas to the class, including the visual representations, so that students have more examples to get their ideas flowing.
- Differentiated Instruction: Teachers could set a minimum number of required symbols for the students to create while comparing.
- Differentiated Instruction: Teachers could copy a few sheets of symbols and place captions under each one so that students have the choice to create their own or use ideas that are offered on the sheets. Clip art from the Internet works well.

- Differentiated Instruction: Teachers could give students the choice of another shape. The students could choose a square, a diamond, or an oval, and they could then reflect upon why that shape brought a stronger level of understanding when completing the comparison.
- Differentiated Instruction: Students could move from a two-dimensional circle to a three-dimensional sphere. Students could tap into other dimensions of symbolism utilizing this adaptation.
- Interdisciplinary Instruction: This assignment is very versatile, so characters do not need to be from fiction. The Mandala can be used to show the differences between countries, between leaders, and so on. The assignment allows students to go beyond use of the word and transcend into symbolism, which permits a deeper and richer connection that can easily be shared across disciplines.
- Teachers can use the two-character predrawing chart (see Figure 2–5) as a way for students to brainstorm more ideas. Michael suggests students fill the boxes with at least three nouns or adjectives (depending on the box requirements). By pushing students to brainstorm in this way, teachers offer them the chance to find a better connection and symbol while also allowing them the opportunity to change their minds. Students should see this as a rough draft, in which they can experiment with many ideas and then choose the one they like best. By building more choice into the assignment, students are less likely to get trapped with sticking to the first ideas that come to mind.

Q & A

What if students have trouble understanding the concept of filling in the categories on the predrawing chart?

This does happen from time to time. One way to solve this is to model a whole-class Mandala by going through the steps listed in the How to Make It Happen section of this activity. The teacher could use a story the class has previously read and allow the students to choose the characters. The teacher can then guide them in filling out the chart on an overhead and even have them create some of the symbols. Another way is to hand out a predrawing chart that has already been filled out as an example. Either way, modeling will solve most of this problem.

What if the challenge of not understanding the predrawing is limited to only a few students?

	Book Title: Character 1:		Book Title: Character 2:	
Your Name: _____ Your Class: _____	Adjective	Character 1	Adjective	Character 2
Color				
Musical Instrument				
Plant or Animal				
Element (Air, Earth, Water, Fire)				
Letter or Symbol				
Most Meaningful Possession				
Hobby				

FIGURE 2–5. *Two-Character Mandala Predrawing Chart*

If only a handful of students have this challenge, Terry has found success with two options. One is to gather the students into a small group and do the minilesson described in the answer to the previous question. The other is to pair a struggling student with a student who understands the assignment and allow them to work together on halves of the Mandala chart. Students often understand better when a peer explains.

Alternative Book Report

It is important that teachers create assessments that allow students to show that they have read and thought about their books. Some of these assessments are tried-and-true, requiring the same basic information that students have been asked to reproduce since they began to read (character, setting, action, resolution). Alternative Book Reports (ABRs) were born out of the need for students to have a choice in how they showcase the *tried-and-true* as well as the need to allow them to choose an option that naturally appeals to their learning strengths.

Michael first heard of an alternative to the basic book report from Joan Kaywell, professor of education at the University of South Florida. She distributed "91 Ways to Respond to a Book," an open-ended list of different ways that students could share their newfound understandings, which had been previously posted on a National Council of Teachers of English listserv by Anne Arvidson (2004), a phenomenal teacher from Rhode Island. (See the appendix for the original list.)

Michael found a treasure chest of engaging assignments but fell into the trap of simply handing out the complete list to his sixth-grade English students, saying, "Here is a list of ninety-one ways you can possibly show that you have read a book. Choose one option and come into class in a week and share your alternative with the class." Unfortunately, the list, although a wonderful resource for teachers, had not originally been written so each alternative was completely equal in weight, requirements, and time required to complete the task. Therefore, giving students too much choice among unequal alternatives led to disastrous results. Since that initial trial by fire, Michael has bent and twisted some of the original options to suit the needs of his students, and he has also allowed the students to do the same. When students' needs for choice are balanced with their need for creativity, expression, equity, and fairness, pure magic can happen in the classroom.

Michael's Experience

April always went above and beyond on every assignment. It seemed to disturb her sensibilities to just follow the directions as stated, so when she found out that there was an option to create a board game that would showcase her knowledge of the book *Lullaby*, by Sarah Dessen, I knew she would go all out. The assignment as I wrote it up stated the following:

> Create a board game based on the settings, events, and characters in the book you read during this reading contract. Your game must include the following: a game board (at least poster size), clear directions (1/2-page, double-spaced/typed minimum), pieces you move (for example, characters), and events from the story on cards (20 events minimum). You will need to teach the class how to play so that by playing your game, members of the class will learn what happened in your book.

On the day the students began to present their Alternative Book Reports, April went first. She had meticulously spray-painted her game board onto a queen-sized bedsheet. Every student's eyes bulged as she unraveled it onto the middle of the carpeted classroom floor. April displayed her penchant for the artistic and totally wowed the class with her painstaking detail for each game square. She picked students to play her game, and they themselves became the game pieces. As they rolled a huge paper die and moved to different squares, they learned more about the book's characters, settings, and actions. April clearly showed that she had read, understood, and thought about her book.

April had a twin sister, Adrienne, who thoroughly enjoyed trying to one-up her sister, but in the end, they both just enjoyed the challenge of coming up with something their eighth-grade class had never seen before. Not wanting to be outdone, Adrienne had an alternative for her book report as well. She had taken advantage of the opportunity to read a book with someone else in the class, and they had chosen to read something other than a novel. Instead, she and Colin had read *The Joy of Signing*, by Lottie L. Riekehof, a book about learning American Sign Language. When they looked at the choices available to them, the board game was the farthest from their minds. Instead they took advantage of the free choice option that allowed students to bring an idea to me and then work out the details of the assignment to ensure that each student in class basically had an equal amount of work for this assignment.

The directions for the free choice option were as follows:

> A New Alternative: Come up with details of an Alternative Book Report that has yet to be presented. The details of your Alternative Book Report must be typed and turned in for review on or before _____ [due date]. You will be given the OK or be asked to modify your request

on that day. It would be a good idea to tell me your idea as soon as possible. Make sure to explain all details of your assignment, itemizing what the requirements will be so that you may earn the highest grade.

Adrienne and Colin were both into scrapbooking as well as the mathematical intricacies of pop-up books, so they decided to create a pop-up book that showed their newfound knowledge. The book first detailed in writing why they wanted to be able to learn the manual alphabet as well as the basics of the language, and then as each page was turned, it taught the class how to *say* three sentences, word for word, in this new language. Though three sentences may not seem all that much after reading an entire book on a completely new language, the way that they decided to show and then teach the class obviously demonstrated the deep reflection and transfer of knowledge that had taken place while reading and creating their book report.

But not every student is an April or an Adrienne.

Mary Ellen had a flair for the dramatic, and she was one of those students who has a natural sense of things. She was the type of student who, from the moment I walked in the room, knew my mood based solely on what I was wearing, how quickly I was walking, and the expression on my face.

When Mary Ellen saw the option for a new alternative, she was the first one to come to me after class with an idea. She wanted to make a movie, and she already knew the most important scenes to capture on film. Mary Ellen had also taken advantage of reading her outside novel with other students, so she had a built-in cast. It was perfect.

Well, not really.

The other students, Frank and Jim, were the type of students who just want to have a good time, so when Mary Ellen suggested that the three of them create a movie together for their ABR, they were all for it. By the time the day of the ABR presentations came, I had lost sight of the fact that Mary Ellen had wanted to create the movie. Therefore, when it was her group's turn to present, I instantly remembered the joy in her step and on her face when she bounced up to me with her original idea and wondered why she was now obviously disappointed about something. Her entire body slumped and galumphed as she slowly made her way to me with the videotape limp in her hand.

"What's up?" I asked.

"This movie is horrible." She just looked at her partners, rolled her eyes, and shuffled by me to the videotape player.

I looked over at Frank and Jim, and they were organizing the class into rows in front of the television. They seemed to have their usual spunk and drive about them, and they were smiling when Frank said, "OK, guys, you are going to love this movie."

Jim chimed in, "Dude, we should have brought popcorn."

Looking back at Mary Ellen, I could see only her back, but she obviously took in a large breath and let out a long sigh.

The video did show important parts of the book, and the class did love the movie. Unfortunately, they loved it because it was so horrible. Frank and Jim had not taken the assignment seriously, and throughout the filming of the project, they could not stop laughing. Also, arguments on how the scene should go were caught on tape, and Frank had obviously not read the book. He continually changed dialogue and action in the scene because he thought it would be better the way he did it instead of sticking to what actually occurred in the book. The plot had an alien race slowly take over suburbia, and the teenagers were the only ones to know the dangers. Mary Ellen's vision had been *Alien* meets *The X-Files*, and Frank and Jim had more of an *Animal House*–meets–*Plan 9 from Outer Space* idea.

Each member of the group had to write up a detailed explanation as to what he or she had contributed to the end product, and though I had asked them to do this in advance and have it ready on the same day of the ABR presentation, I asked each of them to redo that part of the assignment. I wanted them to focus on their contributions to the success of this assignment. I said, "Rewrite your explanation, but make sure to detail everything I saw on tape. How helpful were each of you with making this assignment the best it could be? Did you read the book? Did you help map out each scene? In what way did you contribute to this project? Make sure you are honest about your answers because I have you on tape."

As expected, Mary Ellen had done the lion's share of the work, and Jim had helped out with some of the initial planning. Frank had read about half of the book and had tried to take advantage of the group by playing along, but his sense of play had gotten the better of him. Frank's playing then rubbed off on Jim, and the filming became a catastrophe.

Good did come from this assignment in that class because the students all had a firsthand account of how each individual who works on an Alternative Book Report is held accountable. The idea that group work means one person does the work and the rest of the group tags along and earns the same grade is a practice of the past. In this case, Mary Ellen earned a high grade for her role in the assignment, and both Frank and Jim had to submit another report to prove that they did indeed read the book.

The rest of the class learned valuable lessons as well. In a safe atmosphere, they knew that they would be offered the ability to work with others if that was something that they desired. However, they also learned that individual accountability was a must and that it would be upheld. Lastly, they learned that in any given situation, they could control only themselves, and this lesson will stay with Mary Ellen for quite some time.

Alternative Book Reports have given students the choice to show what they have learned in a way that feels most comfortable to them. Within each assignment, there will be challenges and obstacles, whether from the outside or from internal drive. Either way, these assignments allow students to showcase what they truly know.

How to Make It Happen

1. Teachers need to decide on the book or books that the students will be reporting on first. In Michael's class, he usually assigns these reports for the students to do outside of class (see section on Reading Contracts earlier in this chapter).
2. Deciding on the number of options that will be offered as well as their requirements is the next step. When planning these offerings, teachers might incorporate the idea of multiple intelligences (MIs) (verbal/linguistic, logical/mathematical, musical/rhythmic, bodily/kinesthetic, visual/spatial, interpersonal, intrapersonal, and naturalist), as expressed by psychologist Howard Gardner (1993) in his book *Frames of Mind*. MIs not only speak to students' need to express themselves in a way that is a natural strength but also allow students to stretch into areas in which they need to be nurtured or given more experience. "Using a wide range of instructional strategies allows us not only to reach more students, and to stretch all the intelligences, it allows students to make links across the intelligences . . . the meaning is more fully developed, and the associative links are made across the intelligences, enriching the learning and the students' intellectual development" (Kagan and Kagan 1998, 9.5). When given a choice, students will generally gravitate toward an assignment that they have had success with in the past or one that has elements within it that they find fun or a challenge.
3. Every teacher brings his or her own talents to a classroom, but sometimes he or she might lean more toward writing assignments or more toward art-filled projects. Michael is very verbal (ask anyone who knows him personally), and he has a tendency to offer many verbal

assignments. At the same time, Michael has a strong musical side to his personality, though he rarely thinks of a musical alternative for his English students to use to showcase their understandings. Finding a balance between what comes naturally to the teacher and what the students need to practice or be exposed to is essential. If teachers lean too heavily on any one skill throughout the year and neglect to expose their students to all facets of English/language arts, the students will receive unequal opportunities to learn and grow. An important step in the creation of ABRs is finding this balance that allows students to shine at what they are naturally adept at as well as push and stretch their talents so that they might grow in many areas.

4. The teacher should hand out the assignment well in advance. Students will need ample time to plan and execute most ABRs, so the more time, the better. Whenever possible, Michael hands out the ABR assignment at the same time that the students are choosing their books so that they can be thinking right away about the ABR choice that will work best for the book they decide to read.

5. Within the directions of the assignment, it is a good idea for teachers to incorporate a brainstorming deadline or a halfway point. This allows students to show that they have been working on the ABR, and teachers can decide how much of the assignment students need to show by that point. A brainstorming deadline can require students to show their thinking about what they will incorporate into the assignment. A halfway point can require the students to show one-half of the assignment to prove that they are doing a bit of the assignment at a time. Trial and error will allow each teacher to decide if these parts of the assignment are helpful to herself as well as to the students. Examples of ABRs beyond those already shared include the following:

-   *Novel Town Tour*—You are the tour conductor for the town in which your story was set. During your tour describe the homes, the characters, and the important places where specific events occurred in your book. Type (double-spaced) a three-page script and draw the town on poster board. Your guided tour through the streets of your town must be between three and four minutes in length. Get into your part; through your performance, make people want to read this book.

-   *Moviemaker*—Write a *pitch* to a producer explaining why your novel would make a great movie. Include a cast of characters and the professional actors (a minimum of six) that you would choose to play the parts. Make sure to explain the special effects, big stunts, music, and location of the film (at least two pages, typed and double-spaced). This is a persuasive *pitch*. You must use details from your book and explain in depth why you want to do what you want to do. Please include one poster to portray what the movie billboard might look like. Avoid reproducing the book cover.

6. Presentation of ABRs to an audience is an important step in the process. When students know that there is an audience for their work beyond the teacher, they can gear their presentation to that broader audience. Dependent upon the number of assignments offered, the number of students, and the time available in a teacher's curriculum, presentations may take one class period or many. Teachers will need to plan how they want students to best show their work. Part of this planning can be done during Steps 2 and 3 when teachers are deciding the requirements of each assignment.

ABRs provide students with varying amounts of choice. Teachers may decide to narrow the choices available to make students experience a particular type of ABR but incorporate elements in the project that will allow students to make it their own. Other circumstances might have students choose from a short list of ABRs so that students can work to their strengths. No matter what the teacher's goals, when thoughtfully used, ABRs allow students to have a tremendous amount of control over how they respond to a text.

Adaptations

- Teachers may choose to do only one alternative at first. This limits the students' choice but still gives everyone the opportunity to do something different. Novelty is the spice of a classroom.
- As shown in Michael's Experience, more than one student can work together to create an ABR. For example, if two students read Gordon Korman's *No More Dead Dogs*, and they chose to do the board game, all the requirements—size of board, number of cards, number of rules—would double. In this case, it might also be appropriate to add an extra element to the ABR in addition to increasing the requirements; and this going above and beyond is often suggested. See Beth and Cori's example in Figure 2–6.
- After students have done a few ABRs, the teacher may want to give

FIGURE 2–6. *Beth and Cori's Alternative Book Report Game*

them the opportunity to create their own assignments. Both the movie and the pop-up book were assignments that students came up with on their own. Teachers must be comfortable with giving students this much choice as well as building plenty of time into the process. Though the students are the ones to come up with the initial idea, the teacher is the one who sets the requirements of these alternatives because only the teacher will know what is equitable. For example, if the students want to create a movie, they should provide a script. That script should detail a certain number of scenes as well as contain the elements of setting, characters, dialogue, lighting, camera angles, special effects, and so on. Each ABR has specific requirements that take into account the amount of work as well as the time needed to complete it.

- ABRs could be shared within teams of four, with many teams presenting simultaneously. This is a safe way for students to get used to sharing with a smaller group of students before getting in front of an entire class. If teachers circulate between groups and listen to each one for basics in content and requirements, they can get a good sense of each presentation. This also shows that the students are the most important audience rather than the teacher. If projects are presented this way, teachers will have to spend more time outside of class looking at each part of the assignment, but they may save time in class.

- A game board could be created by the entire class after reading a class novel. Each student would be in charge of a square on the board, and the class as a whole could create the board's layout, the rules of the game, and how students would have to use information from the novel to play. Fun for all ages!

- The game board idea could also require a decorated box beyond just a container to hold the pieces and the board. The box could have to open up and become a part of the game, or students could be required to incorporate marketing ideas that board game manufacturers utilize to entice kids to buy their games.

- Interdisciplinary Instruction: ABRs can be utilized for nonfiction books as well in connection with any other discipline. Both social studies and math have plenty of figures that students could read about and then report their findings on in this unique way. Only the teacher's and students' imagination limits how far this type of response to reading can go.

- Teachers who have ESE students in their classes may consider waiting to hand out the ABR requirements until the students are halfway into their books—engrossed in their texts—and then use that excitement to prompt a response.

Q & A

How are ABRs graded?

Michael uses a very basic rubric that gives credit for the completion of the assignment as well as the depth of understanding of the book. More credit is given to students who go above and beyond the expectations, and less credit is given to those that show a more basic or limited understanding of the book.

Is it possible to fool a teacher by doing an ABR?

Yes it is. Not all teachers have read every book out there, so if a teacher is offering students the opportunity to read a book that he or she has yet to read, then cheating is possible. If a student is caught cheating, that becomes an opportunity to learn lessons other than those already on the curriculum or lesson plans for that week. Michael has had students call other students on being more truthful about their work. One student presented a newspaper front page describing the major events of *Harry Potter and the Prisoner of Azkaban*. Many in the class had read the book, so when the student presented only half of the book as the entire work, there was an uproar from the class. Students and adults alike have a strong sense of fairness and equity.

What if a student's presentation of the material is poor, but the assignment he has created is solid?

That is something that each teacher will need to decide. Is this assignment a reading assignment with specific guidelines and goals, or is this more of a speaking, listening, and viewing assignment geared to a presentation grade? Could it be both? Michael opts for a slant more toward a reading assignment at the beginning of the year and adds more weight to presentation skills such as projection, enunciation, and stance as the year progresses.

Six-Million-Dollar Testing—Better and Stronger

Michael has had the opportunity to help teach a college-level curriculum and instruction class, and one activity had these curriculum students and soon-to-be teachers talk about what they thought of when someone mentioned the word *test*. An overwhelming percentage mentioned stress, anxiety, types of required tests, and late nights with caffeine. Rarely did anyone bring up *fun* or *real-world application*. When Michael asked, "Why?" they invariably shrugged their shoulders.

"Tests just aren't fun," one blurted out.

"Because no teacher I have ever had thought about me when making a test. It's always about the teacher, not the student," another said.

Michael asked in reply, "Is that the type of teacher you want to be?"

All teachers constantly look for ways to make their practice better and stronger. The type of testing described here, unlike many types of tests teachers traditionally use, offers ways to reexamine through testing what students know and how they show that knowledge.

Traditional testing, often referred to as analytical literacy, is based on the belief that there is only one answer, one point of view, one reason that the author did as he or she did, and it is the requirement of the reader to extract that information by any means possible. In former United States poet laureate Billy Collins' (2003) poem "Introduction to Poetry," the author invites all to play within poetry:

> . . . drop a mouse into a poem
> and watch him probe his way out,
> or walk inside a poem's room
> and feel the walls for a light switch . . .

However, Collins ends the poem on a note that seems almost predictable and agonizing for literature as a whole.

> . . . But all they want to do
> is tie the poem to a chair with rope
> and torture a confession out of it.
> They begin beating it with a hose
> to find out what it really means.

As Robert Frost spoke about his poem "Stopping by Woods on a Snowy Evening," he said, "that one I've been more bothered with than anybody has ever been with any poem in just pressing it for more than it should be pressed for. It means enough without being pressed" (Cook 1974, 52). He was tired of *academics* taking the hose and beating and torturing the meaning out of his poor beleaguered poem.

Some teachers use analytical literacy because it is all they have ever known, copying what their experience has shown them. Taking the stance that there is only one interpretation stifles the creativity of students and teachers alike, and when teachers hold fast to this approach as ideal, literature can get trapped in a straightjacket and sucked dry of all the possibilities that each student could bring to it.

A more interactive approach to reading asks students to bring themselves as well as others into the reading of the text to analyze and critique a text's language, format, point of view, and even intent. This approach, often identified as critical literacy, allows each reader to bring a different set of experiences, beliefs, and thoughts to a text and allows all to experience a text individually as well as collectively. Further, many teachers have held to the belief that students can always have an opinion about a text as long as they can back it up with clear evidence directly from that text and the world around them.

Teachers also believe that the reason that students read literature is to learn more about themselves and the world around them, to examine life with different lenses, and to question what they see daily against ideas other than those supported by their own communities. With this framework, Michael took the idea of what the individual brings to a text and broadened it to a whole-class discussion. He thought that if he had the right question and a meaty text that allowed for varying points of view, the students could prove they read, understood, and thought critically about that text. A culminating project for the eighth-grade summer reading unit lent itself perfectly to this goal.

Michael's Experience

Jeffery was new to the school, but he had made his presence known early. His mouth was rapid-fire, and his behavior landed him in the main office quickly and often. But when Jeffery found out that I planned on having a classroom discussion about the summer reading book, *Ender's Game,* by Orson Scott Card, his behavior straightened up quickly. He wanted his voice to be heard.

Ender's Game details the rise and conquests of young Ender Wiggin, the only hope for the future of the human race. Throughout the book, Ender is confronted by those who want to hurt him in some way, and Ender often ends each conflict with a definitive message to all those that might try to hurt him again: think twice about doing so.

Therefore, I posed this question to my eighth-grade students: "When do you believe that hurting someone until he or she is no longer a threat is right and/or justified? Make sure to back up your answer with examples from the book and life around you."

I allowed students to create their tests at home and I encouraged collaboration. Other students, siblings, parents, newspapers, magazines, and the Internet were all valid collaborators. Each would bring a different perspective to the question, and then students had to negotiate meaning with the evidence that they had collected. I warned students to make sure to submit their own thoughts and their own words for this assignment. Though collaboration would be permitted, collusion would not.

On the day the take-home test was due, Jeffery, usually a lackluster performer when it came to turning in his work, gripped his well-creased and weathered test in his hand. He beamed, "I have my work today, Mr. V."

"That's great!" I answered back. "I can't wait to hear what you have to say."

I asked the students in Jeffery's class to assign themselves a number between zero and one hundred. If they were a pacifist and believed that violence was never an option, even if that meant that someone could hurt them and their family for doing nothing but breathing and they would not retaliate, then they should choose zero. If instead they thought they should retaliate not only when they had been personally hurt but also that it was necessary to hunt down and destroy all of those that might ever eventually pose a threat to them, then they should choose one hundred. Obviously, if there were circumstances that fell between those two extremes and students felt that their answer was more of a mixture of the two, they should choose a number somewhere in between.

Not surprisingly, Jeffery chose one hundred.

As the conversation started, Jeffery was antsy to get his turn to speak, rocking back and forth on his chair like it was wired to a low-voltage car battery, and when it came time for him to speak, his words came with a flourish: "Nuke 'em. Nuke 'em all. America is the best nation on the planet, and we need to get everyone on the same page. If they don't want to tow the line, nuke 'em."

The class laughed heartily at his enthusiasm, but as the conversation continued on that first day, the laughter died down and was replaced with worried looks that seemed to ask, "Who is this new kid, and why is he so violent?"

The conversation went on for three days (three forty-five-minute periods), and as the evidence from the rest of the class started to pile up from the book, the law, current events, injustices in the world and at school, as well as personal accounts of perceived and genuine threats, Jeffery's position began to soften. He no longer vibrated in his chair, ready to pounce on anybody who would oppose him. Instead, he began to listen, taking in what others said, accepting their points of view as valid.

On the third day, Jeffery asked, "Mr. V., can I change my number?"

"Of course you can."

"OK." He straightened up in his chair. "I have been listening to all of you, and now I change my number to twenty." Jeffery went on for the next five minutes, sequentially agreeing or disagreeing with points made by many students, forging a new answer to the take-home test he had originally completed. This one assignment brought Jeffery's real personality into the classroom as opposed to the first-days-of-school tough-guy persona that he had been portraying up to this point.

At the end of three days of discussion, students from each class asked something that was totally new to me. They asked to go back and retool their original test answers so that they could change them to reflect what they now felt. Having listened to other points of view, both differing from and mirroring their original ideas, many students wanted the opportunity to adjust their answers. They had learned something more about the subject and felt that their original answers were no longer accurate representations of their feelings and understandings.

I hadn't planned on it, but I smiled and said, "Of course you can."

Testing does not need to be a paper-and-pencil, anxiety-driven, *I am going to get you* situation. I am so excited to have had this type of *test* literally evolve in front of my eyes because it brought out the personality of my classes as well as their humanness. This is why we read literature.

How to Make It Happen

1. Teachers must choose a piece of literature that has enough substance, or *meat,* to it to allow students to sink their teeth in and really chew on it. A good choice would be something that relates to the current world around them or something that deals with a pressing issue in their own lives.
2. Teachers must ask a question that is just as open-ended as needed to bring about a wide range of answers that can be supported by both the text and the world itself.
3. Teachers pass out a *take-home test* with all directions about the question, the product, the grading rubric (see Figure 2–7), and the discussion. Including all of this information up front allows the students to be well aware of what to expect. The time allowed to complete the test will be up to the teacher. Michael usually schedules the assignment over four days or over a long weekend.

     The *Ender's Game* take-home test stated the following:

*   Please answer the question below. Be ready to discuss and defend your answer during class discussion.
*   *Fact:* The reason we read literature is to learn more about ourselves and the world around us.
*   *Discussion:* We have all read *Ender's Game,* penned by Orson Scott Card. During this piece of literature, Card brings up (through Ender's actions) the idea of hurting someone until he or she is no longer a threat (you remember what happened to Stilson and Bonzo).
*   During your lifetime, our own country has made some decisions on this very subject. Even in today's justice system there are laws in place that take this very stance.
*   *Question:* When do you believe that hurting someone until he or she is no longer a threat is right and/or justified? Make sure to back up your answer with examples from life around you and the book.

- *Utilize:* You may use the following as resources: Your copy of *Ender's Game,* each other, your parents, your thoughts and brainstorming, newspapers, magazines, and the Internet.
- *Product:* Turn in a product that shows your understanding of the answer, the book, the short story, and the world around you.
- *Goal:* To see how you think. Content is most important for this test.

4. Teachers need to make sure that they schedule enough time for the discussions. Depending on the size of the class, the meatiness of the subject matter, and the students themselves, a teacher needs to allow for some lengthy discussions. Michael's discussions have averaged three days each with twenty students in each class.

5. Teachers can have the students select a number on a number line between zero and one hundred to represent their views on the subject at hand. This helps to concretize their position at the beginning of the discussion and also allows for a quick reference point so that they might understand where someone *stands* on the issue as well as decide if they need to move themselves to another point on the sliding scale of that issue.

6. The teacher must be the moderator of the discussion. If a subject or strand of discussion is barely breathing, the teacher must be able to switch gears and steer the conversation to another idea. Michael has specific rules that are in place during *discussion mode.* These rules include the following:

- All eyes are on the one speaker who has the floor.
- Use hands at another time. We are having a discussion, so be patient and appropriate throughout.
- All opinions are accepted both verbally and nonverbally.
- Use the names of those whose opinions you are building upon (I agree with Bob's point about . . . , but I disagree with Tom because. . . .).
- When speaking to the group, give proper eye contact. You are having a conversation with all of us.

7. The teacher also must take a backseat and allow the students to drive the discussion. If students know that the teacher will just come in and tell them how wrong they are and how they should have answered the question, the reason for completing the assignment is lost. The teacher

Score 6—Exemplary (excellent or ideal) Reading Performance

Showing their insight into their own learning of *Ender's Game*, readers are able to construct and reflect on their own meaning making. Readers do this by filling in gaps by making assumptions about what is unsaid as well as about what was personally learned. Literal and figurative meanings are understood and explained easily. By connecting the book and the world around them, readers are able to reflect on and express their own ideas. Readers may agree or disagree with the teacher's ideas, but they are able to use reasoning to explain their thoughts.

Score 5—Discerning (sharp and perceptive) Reading Performance

This performance shows good understandings of the book and world around them, especially about subtle hints that most readers leave out. Some meanings may lack some creativity, insight, or reflection, but they are thoroughly presented. Gaps of understanding were filled in by meaningful assumptions, and meanings explained are made by exploring their understandings of what they have learned.

Score 4—Thoughtful Reading Performance

Readers show they understand the meanings and possible contradictions in the book and world around them by making reasonable and believable connections to their own experience and knowledge. Some explanation, though purposeful, is present, and ideas are accepted as is. One or more meanings may be shown, but readers have some trouble expressing or explaining their own opinions.

Score 3—Literal (factual and exact) Reading Performance

Readers show a very literal level of understanding of their learning and lack depth in their answers. A sense of the book and the world around them may be present, but it is simplistic and plain.

Score 2—Limited Reading Performance

Readers show some understandings of the book and the world around them that are obvious and completely on the surface. They may start a good idea and then derail to connections that are truly off the tracks.

Score 1—Minimal Reading Performance

Meaning is lost to the students as to what they have learned because only some parts of the book or the world around them make any sense. Everything that is said is vague and unsupported.

FIGURE 2–7. Ender's Game *Take-Home Test—Rubric*

should require students to back up their points of view and require equal access to the discussion floor. This allows for a successful in-class critical literacy discussion.

Six-Million-Dollar Testing provides teachers with options for student response to a text that are limitless in the amount of choice offered. Students have the opportunity to negotiate and renegotiate meanings, to change their stance on the theme explored through the text, and to choose to use various sources beyond the original text to ensure their understanding. Finally, aspects of Six-Million-Dollar Testing allow students to decide how they will respond. The product, for example, can be anything that shows that the student understands the original text.

Adaptations

- Discussions can take place with any form of literature. We used the novel *Ender's Game* as an example, but many novels, short stories, and poetry lend themselves very well to a critical literacy discussion.
- Teachers can offer extra credit to students who bring in a signed note stating that they have had at least a thirty-minute conversation with a parent or guardian about the content of this test. This promotes a critical literacy discussion at home and allows students to shape their views before the classroom discussion. (Jeffrey N. Golub initially gave Michael this idea.)
- Teachers may or may not offer the opportunity for students to change their test answers based upon the class discussions (the Jeffery proposal). The tests that Michael has read after he has given the students the opportunity to change their original perceptions have shown a deeper connection to the issues, the text, and the world around them. Isn't that the entire point of *testing* literature in the first place?
- Interdisciplinary Instruction: If a district, school, or team within the school has essential questions that bind instruction for a unit, a trimester, or a semester, utilizing those questions and requiring students to give examples from all of their classes would allow students to see the interconnectedness of the curriculum as well as allow teachers to see if what they had planned for the students to experience is actually happening.
- For the language impaired, a graded whole-class discussion may prove to be a bit too difficult. Instead of giving a grade for participation during the discussions, teachers could have students turn in a visual repre-

sentation of the ideas expressed, bring in some research that they find that supports the views discussed, or clip out an entire article on a current event that correlates with their own thoughts.

Q & A

Does a teacher give a grade for the discussion?

Michael does give a discussion score because it is a skill for a student to speak her mind, address a large group of people, and get a point across and support it with solid evidence. During the conversation, Michael keeps track of who has spoken and how well he does so. In his experience, because the students know ahead of time that they will be graded for this contribution, many make sure to earn their grade. Others need to be reminded to share their opinions, and the class as a whole often reminds those students that still need to share.

What if a student decides to stay silent during the discussion period but had a wonderful take-home test with great ideas throughout?

These are two different grades. The take-home test product receives a score based upon the rubric, and the in-class discussion receives a grade based upon participation, the examples a student gives, and how well the student follows directions during the discussion.

What does Michael mean by product *in his* Ender's Game *take-home test directions?*

If a teacher states *essay* within the directions of an assignment, all the students will turn in an essay. If instead the teacher asks for a *product*, the doors can open for the students to think outside of the ordinary and turn in products that they will enjoy creating. Students will be clear about their products and their grades as long as the teacher continuously directs students back to the grading rubric by stating, "In completing this product, as long as all of the requirements of the rubric are met, the student should be able to obtain the desired grade."

Isn't it cheating if you allow students to talk to their peers, their siblings, and their parents before they turn in the test?

No. The aim for all students is to have them think about what they have learned and negotiate meaning from that newfound information. Part of negotiating meaning is allowing for prior knowledge and being cognizant of the world. If peers, siblings, and parents can add a richer dimension to what has already happened in the classroom as well as in their minds, the students are better for it.

Further Resources

Collins, Billy. 2002. *Sailing Alone Around the Room*. New York: Random House.

Rosenblatt, Louise. 1996. *Literature as Exploration*. New York: Modern Language Association of America.

People Fair

Local, state, and national conferences are the best places to keep abreast of the latest in English education, to make lifelong contacts that foster and challenge thinking and learning, and to find inventive activities that engage students. Michael was lucky to find one activity, People Fair, at the Florida Council of Teachers of English fall conference in 1998. This unit plan originated with Virginia White of Fernandina Beach Middle School, and Michael has since tweaked it for his own audience, as all teachers should do to fit their own situation.

The unit involves students researching someone who has made a positive impact on the world and then completing ten assignments in six to eight weeks that showcase their newfound knowledge. The premise involves students having control over their own research, reading, writing, artistic, and computer skills. Eventually each student becomes the person he has researched for a fair that honors these men and women and their accomplishments.

The People Fair became an inventive way to look at a biography and brought life to the ordinary book report. Instead of dreading to read an assigned, dry, boring biography, students look forward to becoming people they are interested in because they have had the choice of whom to study. If students are excited, the products will be astonishing.

Michael's Experience

I originally tried the People Fair with my sixth-grade classes and no sooner had I announced the People Fair as the trimester's research-based project than the questions began to roll in. "What's a People Fair? Read a what? What's a biography? Is this going to be fun?"

I only smiled and said, "You're going to love it."

Students first needed to choose a role model or hero about whom they were interested in learning more. Knowing about interests of sixth graders, I thought it was inevitable that students would have some of the same heroes and/or interests, so I decided to tell the students, "Make sure to bring in a minimum of three names. Discuss this fair with your parents, your friends, and your family, and then decide whom you would like to study for the next six to eight weeks."

It did turn out that there were students who had the same first choice, so I let those students decide among themselves who would research whom. I literally sent students outside my classroom with their lists in hand and let them discuss their choices. It turned out that each student came back happy with his or her choice.

Some students did have to make tough but informed decisions about whom to study. One student agonized and then finally decided to choose someone other than his first choice. This young man was very interested in learning about Oprah Winfrey, her life, and her positive influence on the world, but he was uncomfortable with the idea that he would have to dress, act, and speak like a middle-aged woman onstage. On the other hand, because of one young lady's interest in science, she felt comfortable enough to choose to learn about and become Albert Einstein. She had fun finding a large white wig and listening and watching archived tapes so that she might get his voice and mannerisms down. I was impressed with how smoothly this part of the process turned out.

Subjects chosen ranged from Michael Jordan to Mother Teresa (Figure 2–8). I was impressed at the range and diversity of the subjects and even learned about the runner Steve Prefontaine, the Confederate spy Rose O'Neal Greenhow, and the horseman Mark Todd. It blew my mind that sixth-grade students even knew who some of these people were, let alone wanted to read about them, complete ten assignments about them, and then actually become them in front of an audience.

After their subject had been finalized, students had to find and read a print biography about that person. When I was first planning this unit, I did not realize that there were biographies and then there were *biographies*. When I was younger, biographies were always found in the library in the biography section, but the genre had changed since I'd last read one for class back in the 1970s.

There are plenty of books that can be called biographies. These are thrown together in quick fashion based upon the recent fascinations of teenagers or preteens or even those to drum up support for political figures. These biographies are easily accessible and are usually located in drug or grocery stores right next to the "I had Bigfoot's baby" tabloids. They are written on a very low reading level and often contain shoddy information.

FIGURE 2–8. *Carol Ann as Mother Theresa*

Therefore, I was shocked when my sixth graders came in with books rang-
ing from texts that would make college students cringe because of their
sheer size to light pamphlets that had only a few three-syllable words in
them. It was a trial-and-error period that could have been avoided, but
eventually all students found books that would allow them to complete the
assignments. I know now that if the requirements of the biography are clearly stated and examples and nonexamples are given, all confusion can be
avoided.

Each of the ten assignments that students have to complete requires
them to go back to their own research and produce information. The design
of the order of assignments requires them to delve deeper into their subjects'
lives with the completion of each one.

The first People Fair was marvelous. The sixth grade took over the
entire gym for the day and presented their monologues three different times
to elementary children, middle school students, and parents. After the
event, the sixth graders shared a great idea: they suggested taking some time
the day before the presentations so each student could see each other's
props, costumes, and other displayed assignments. The students felt they
missed the opportunity to interact with their peers and see what the other
students had accomplished.

The pride and detail students placed into each assignment showcased the vast amount of learning and excitement that they had brought to the fair. They were so impressed with not only their peers but also what they themselves had accomplished in eight weeks' time.

During that first year, I tried to have the students both read the book and complete all ten of the assignments at once. Because of this, I ran out of time. Students did finish the first three assignments (birth certificate, letter, and T-shirt) with ease and then could not get the time line or any other assignment finished for weeks because of the enormity of the request of more detailed information. This, of course, pushed everything else back, delaying the original fair date by two weeks.

I love this unit of study. Students are engaged and excited about learning about people that they themselves choose to learn more about. Students are invested from the beginning and each assignment allows them to learn even more about their favorite heroes or role models. I wish all units of study engendered this much love and excitement for learning.

How to Make It Happen

Usually this section is just the step-by-step directions on how to do an activity in the classroom. Because there are ten different assignments wrapped up in this unit of study, Michael thought it would be better to incorporate the directions with some of his experiences so that each direction would be accompanied by good concrete examples.

Choosing a Subject: Anyone is fair game as long as the drive to learn is there. Michael's school did place the students' focus on those that had made positive rather than negative contributions to society. These are the guidelines Michael gives to the students:

1. Find a print biography on the person you want to research.
2. The person must have had a positive influence on or contribution to humanity.
3. You yourself must be sincerely interested in learning about this person.
4. You must also feel comfortable in eventually transforming yourself into this person.
5. Each student must have his or her own, unique research subject.

From the beginning of the unit, students have a vested interest in what they study and appreciate their choice of subject. With the above guidelines, the students know before they make their choice that they will be studying a person so closely that they will eventually be required to become that person in dress, speech, and mannerisms.

Subject Doubles: Teachers should require students to bring in *at least* three subject names so that each student has a unique research subject. If teachers inevitably will have more than one People Fair because of the number of students or decide to run a smaller version in individual classes, they should make sure that each fair has its own unique set of personalities to avoid having two Michael Jordans or three Brett Favres in the same room.

Choice of Biography: There are many books out there that are called biographies. Before students begin looking for their books, it is important for the teacher to show them examples of the types of biographies that will be accepted for this assignment. Based on the audience, teachers might accept biographies that are found in grocery stores. If teachers make that decision before they require students to bring these books to class, the opportunity for smooth sailing is possible.

Reading the Biography: This should be planned in advance of the time that will be allotted for the assignments and the fair. It is easier to have students read their books and then return to them to find details rather than have them read the books and complete assignments at the same time. Only the first three of the ten assignments can be completed with minimal information. If teachers can work it out so that the books are read beforehand, they may circumvent some backlog related to completing assignments that require very specific and detailed information.

Time Management: To say that Michael struggled with the time management aspects of this fair is a giant understatement. Teachers must first decide what assignments are right for their audience, and that decision alone will allow them to manage the amount of time they want to dedicate to this unit.

The first three assignments can be completed as students begin to read the book.

Birth Certificate: This assignment requires students to find and present basic information. Where was their subject born? When? To whom? Did she have a different name than the one most people know her as today?

- *Options:* Students can research if their subject would even have had a birth certificate and then decide what it would look like. Students also can add details to their certificate like state or county seals. It is also fun to ask students to bring in a copy of their own birth certificate so that they might decide what to include on the one they must create.

- *Michael's Experience:* Students had a ball trying to find out specific information about their subjects and *giving birth* to them. Knute Rockne, Thomas Edison, and Annie Oakley had weathered pieces of parchment. Julius Caesar had a scroll with pertinent information. I learned Jackie O's, Tiger Woods', and Joan of Arc's real names. My students learned this basic information and taught the rest of us through this assignment.

Letter: For their second assignment, students write a letter that depicts an important time in their subject's life. This assignment, written from the subject's point of view, makes the students begin to think as if they are that person. After the students choose the important event, they write to someone who is important to their person, exhibiting depth of knowledge about their subject. If an extra step is needed to help students choose what to write about, it might be helpful to have the students correlate an important event in their own life with one that was important to their persona. This can make the transition from student to persona a little smoother and allow the students a little leeway in their observations.

- *Michael's Experience:* The letter allowed students to show they knew their subject and what was important in their subject's life. It was a key, initial step that strengthened the idea that the students would eventually transform themselves into their subject. Capturing just the right wording or voice for their letter showed that students really knew their subjects and were beginning to think like them in their writing. For example, Franklin D. Roosevelt explained the reasoning behind entering World War II, and Amelia Earhart explained why she had decided to attempt to fly around the world.

T-Shirt: The last of the first three assignments has the students use their creativity to design a marketable T-shirt that presents the essence of their subject. Color and simplicity of design are important. The assignment is purposely vague to allow for creativity and *out-of-the-box* thinking.

- *Options:* Students can be given a paper T-shirt form to fill in, or students can create actual T-shirts with fabric paint and embellishments.
- *Michael's Experience:* The T-shirt allowed students to be expressive about their subject in a *marketing* sense, and it sparked debate and requests for a more specific definition of the word *essence*, and I tried to be as cryptic as possible. I asked each class, "Is this the same *essence*

they talk about in perfume commercials? Does just a picture of some-one's face capture his or her *essence*? Can you use symbols, words, or sayings?" I wanted to stay away from defining it and showing examples because, in this case, doing so might quash any ingenuity or creativity. As the process continued, I often heard students ask each other, "Would you wear this in public or buy this?" The students eventually showcased symbolism, color representation, and most importantly their own imaginations. John Muir had a Sierra Club insignia, and Wilbur Wright's T-shirt simply shouted, "We <u>can</u> fly!"

The last seven assignments can be completed with greater ease and efficiency after the students have read their biography.

Time Line: Students must research and choose at least fifteen important details about their subject's life. They then need to research and choose at least eight world events that occurred *during* their subject's life. Lastly, to enhance the time line display, five to ten illustrations are also required.

- *Options:* Depending on the number of students in the class and the time dedicated to this assignment, the teacher can adjust the size and requirements to fit the audience and its needs. A small poster that represents this information can be just as effective as a large banner.
- *Michael's Experience:* The time line assignment took the most amount of planning and the longest time to complete because I required that the time line be ten feet long by three feet wide (done on butcher paper) with an attention-getting graphic and the subject's name on the top. This was an interesting choice on my part, but I was copying the People Fair I had been presented instead of looking at each assignment for its worth. It turned out that the attention-getting graphic took the longest amount of time because students had to use the overhead projector to enlarge a graphic and trace it onto their butcher paper. The effect of having an entire school gym papered with more than fifty of these huge time lines was spectacular, but the creation of the product required oodles of time. This must be a personal choice of the teacher. Is it more important to have the *spectacle* or preferable to require that a smaller time line be completed correctly in a timely fashion? If I had to do it all over again, I might choose the smaller version.

Map or Atlas: The students have to identify ten geographical locations that were important to their subject's life and prepare a way to present that information, showcasing the importance of each location.

- *Options:* The teacher can offer copies of maps of the United States and the world and an atlas of individual sections of the world to help students along.
- *Michael's Experience:* By choosing ten important locations in the world on a map or atlas, students made important connections to their social studies class. Most students used poster board and note cards that explained each locality's significance. Some students made an atlas with an appropriate cover and accompanying maps with information inside. One student created something entirely different; he used an actual globe to illustrate how Julius Caesar slowly spread his power in the first century BC.

Venn Diagram: A Venn diagram has two circles that overlap slightly. The student places information and characteristics about herself that is different from her subject in one circle and does the same for her subject in the other. Where the circles overlap, the student must place information and characteristics that she shares with the subject. The Venn diagram helps students compare themselves with their subject, determining what is different as well as the same between them, and it encourages students to find some very personal connections.

- *Michael's Experience:* Students did need to learn about the Venn diagram and how to use it. There are even websites dedicated to teaching visitors about them as well as creating them as a free service. Teachers can go to the Internet and type "Venn diagram" into a search engine to find the website that is the most kid-friendly. Once that initial explanation was complete, this assignment brought home the interconnectedness that students had with their subjects. That information helped define in concrete terms what types of personality traits, ways of dress, or even speech patterns the students would have to change about themselves to give a convincing performance on People Fair day. One student told me after class, "You know, I never thought that I had anything in common with Michael Jordan, but now that I've thought about it, we both strive to do our best at anything we do."

Journal/Diary: The journal assignment asks the students to assume their character's identity and write five diary entries. The entries are to show their person's important life events, including a child's entry with a suitable drawing. The cover has to look like something that that person would own.

- *Options:* The number of journal entries and the requirements of what will be accepted as a journal entry are the areas of this assignment that can be most easily adapted to fit a particular situation. The teacher's audience will determine the requirements here.

- *Michael's Experience:* I stresssed that the students should balance voice, imagination, and creativity with the reality of their person's life while writing these entries. Accomplishing that took some time, and examples helped immensely.

Costume and Props: For the People Fair itself, students need to dress as their subject and bring at least five items that reflect the *flair* and *time* of their subject.

- *Options:* There is no need to do both of these or either of these, so teachers can choose costumes or props or neither. If a fair takes place in a classroom, space can become a factor with too many props. Also, depending on the students, costumes may be too much of a burden to place upon them. The teacher will decide what is most important for his students.
- *Michael's Experience:* Students went all out for this assignment; they rented costumes, sewed costumes from scratch, and made helmets, shields, and the Lombardi trophy from aluminum foil. Priceless sports cards, autographed materials, footballs, basketballs, and even Stephen Hawking's black holes (made from chicken wire) are examples of props that students brought in for the fair. It was a joy to see the smiles and the pride that they had as each came in wanting to share something (if not everything) he or she had created.

Monologue: The monologue assignment requires students to perform a sixty- to ninety-second speech during the People Fair. Students are to assume that the audience is unfamiliar with their character, no matter how famous, so that they show their learning as well as inform their audience.

- *Options:* Time and notes are the teacher's biggest options for this assignment. Will a short memorized piece or a longer notes-driven monologue be required?
- *Michael's Experience:* I cautioned the students to stay away from chronologies for their short monologue on fair day. I required students to start working on their monologue early so that they would be comfortable in front of an audience and speaking into a microphone. The early preparation worked well; Jane Goodall showed poise and conviction in her presentation while Marcus Allen showed his humorous side by making fun of his bald head.

Works Cited Page: This assignment is handed in last, after the fair, and lists all materials that the students used to create the People Fair assignments. All books and websites are required.

- *Michael's Experience:* Turned in after the fair, this was the most traditional of all of the assignments, but it was a perfect opportunity for students to learn the proper format to cite all of the sources that they used for each of the assignments that made the People Fair what it was. It was difficult to go back and do this after the fact, so creating this along the way each time a student finds and uses information would be better in the future.

The Day of the People Fair

This day provides the teacher with the most flexibility. Teachers can overtake the gymnasium or just rearrange the classroom. They can invite other grades from the school, or it can be a private affair for just the students and their parents. The options are limitless.

The People Fair is one of the most choice-laden activities in this chapter. Students have an abundance of people they can study and many choices regarding how they will present each of the activities. Student choice is the basis for this entire unit.

Adaptations

- Completing all ten assignments may not be necessary to showcase student learning. Thinking about multiple intelligences and how students could show their newfound knowledge may reduce the fair down to just a few assignments.
- The People Fair could be a large Alternative Book Report that requires an in-character monologue from each student.
- This type of fair could be offered as extra credit for those students who have a flair for the dramatic.
- To offer a more *safe* performance opportunity, students could videotape their monologue in the school library or at home.
- Requirements specifying which *people* can be chosen could limit options to a particular time period, allowing a specific connection with the social studies program. Students could reenact the signing of the Declaration of Independence, with each student representing a different researched character. A round-table discussion of the effects of World War II on important personalities could occur with American

generals, German leaders, interned Japanese, Jewish survivors, and others.

- Students could each write a biography on someone in their family, and teachers could encourage the family members to come to see how accurately they are portrayed by their student relatives.

- Students could be held accountable for what they see at the People Fair, with a structure that requires the students to listen to those presenting and then match some basic facts about the personalities with their names on a handout. Students really enjoy the one-on-one conversations that they have when interviewing the celebrities as well as the follow-up in their own classrooms to see how well they filled out the form. The fair takes on a special appeal if the teacher allows the audience to interact with the students while they stay in character. The students will need to think more on their feet about what they have learned because they will be interacting with an audience instead of speaking from a script.

- Interdisciplinary Instruction: A People Fair for those key players in any historical time period or event and a People Fair for those people who are important from a particular ethnic background are two ways that this activity could tie disciplines together.

- For many students, including ESE students, the use of a graphic organizer, such as a Who, What, When, Why, Where chart or a Who Am I? web, might be helpful for organizing any information during the People Fair. This will allow a student to go from the concrete to the abstract with greater ease.

- Using a multiple intelligences (MI) approach, students could add many touches to their presentations. They could re-create a dance and need to teach the audience some moves. They could create a song based on the character's life and perform it. They might even paint a picture that their character might have painted as a child. It is extremely important, especially for ESE students, to be able to show that they have acquired knowledge without relying on a rubric that accentuates their disability. Instead, teachers may want to give students an MI checklist before the project begins to gauge where their strengths lie and then create the rubric for which they will be held accountable.

3

Choice in Vocabulary

Building vocabulary is an extension of reading. As we read, we naturally gather words that we come to own through exposure to and engagement with them in context or conversation. No matter where the new words come from, as teachers we need to pass our love of words on to our students. The difficulty lies in the specific pressures that each teacher has when it comes to vocabulary. Some of us have a specifically mandated program that says certain words must be introduced every Monday and tested every Friday. Some of us have the specified program but no one telling us how or when to use it. Others have no specific vocabulary direction at all, but we know that vocabulary development is crucial. With these considerations in mind, this chapter contains activities with adaptations that address a variety of teaching situations.

The first, Vocabulary Contracts, is an approach to use when dealing with a specific program. The contracts allow students to choose how much vocabulary they will take on as well as their tentative grade in advance. The second activity is for those teachers who have more flexibility in their teaching situation. It addresses several ways for teachers to generate vocabulary words for their students and offers students the ability to show their ownership of these words.

Often when students are told that they will be *doing* vocabulary, groans will ooze throughout the classroom. We hope that by infusing choice into the process, the two ideas in this chapter will squelch those groans ever so slightly.

Vocabulary Contract

Vocabulary has become yet another area that standardized tests have quantified, qualified, and categorized, but in the classroom it can be an elusive and sly animal sneaking around in the shadows of the back ally of the classroom. The teachers know it is there, but it would be better if it were caged and fed well so they always would know where it was and would be in full control of the wild beast.

Vocabulary Contracts grew out of Michael's need to individualize the vocabulary program he is required to use. Students come to school with varying abilities to take in and utilize information. New words are acquired by students at completely different times, and creating a system so each student can find success is important. The Vocabulary Contract allows students to choose their level of work over a specific period of time. Students are trusted to be cognizant of their own level of understanding and ability to soak up new information. The contract embodies that trust but contains within it checkpoints to make sure that the student stays on track.

Michael's Experience

I have always thought that students learn vocabulary best through reading. It is through this constant exposure to language that I feel students can best learn and appreciate vocabulary. That being said, few systems or programs allow students to learn vocabulary individually in a classroom setting exclusively through their outside reading. Instead there are many vocabulary programs that have been based on particular vocabulary viewpoints.

One program touts that it has generated college entrance preparation words that are age appropriate for each grade in middle and high school. Students who know these words, the program purports, will do well on entrance exams.

Another program explains that word roots and words associated with these roots are the building blocks of vocabulary. If students memorize these roots, any new word offered to them will be recognizable. Therefore, the students will score well on standardized tests.

My English department decided that the program with college entrance preparation words was the best for our student population. Other local middle and high schools had been using this same program and workbook, and the expectation of our middle school was to prepare students for wherever they might enroll next. This program called for twenty words to be memorized and quizzed per lesson, and there were about fifteen lessons in each workbook. The students completed assignments in a workbook containing the words, their definitions, as well as fill-in-the-blank sentences, synonyms, antonyms, and sentence completion exercises. Students then took quizzes and tests provided by the company that had created the program.

When I first began using this program, all students had to take the same quiz on the same day. This made for a specific routine for me when it came to preparing the students for each quiz. I assigned each of the workbook activities in order, and I required vocabulary flash cards to help students *see* the words in another way. This system was set up for all students to follow without deviation. I found that many students either had trouble keeping up with the requirements of this system or were bored by its repetitiveness, so I decided to create a new system to allow for individualized student growth and learning. The Vocabulary Contract took the regimentation out of the previous method of vocabulary instruction and replaced it with a new set of expectations. The students were now in control of their learning as well as their grade.

I first had to create the contract. I looked at my twelve-week marking period as a whole and decided on the number of words that I thought students should be able to master not only through the workbook exercises, flash cards, and program quizzes but also through writing. I set up a grid that outlined what students had to complete to earn a specific grade. These guidelines detailed how many lessons, quizzes, tests, and writing assignments would be required to earn the grade they were most interested in achieving for the marking period.

The requirement that I deemed most important was the mastery of the words. In the past, students had mastered each of the exercises but then failed the quiz on the same words. Therefore, I created a 90 percent mastery requirement. As long as students earned a 90 percent on each activity, quiz, and test, they were allowed to go on to the next unit. Also, if they earned this percentage on all of their required work within their chosen letter grade, they earned that letter grade for the marking period in vocabulary. See Figure 3–1.

Lastly, I placed a signature requirement upon the contract. Students and their parents would have to sign the contract so that all were in agreement as to the goals for the contract period. This part of the contract was important so that as the marking period continued, I could go back to the contract and remind students of their commitment as well as enlist parental help if needed.

I distributed their contracts at the beginning of the marking period and asked students to take their contract home to discuss it with their parents. They were to choose a letter grade that they wished to attain, based upon what they felt they could accomplish within that time period. If they and their parents were content with the requirements for earning a B in

An expanded vocabulary increases your capacity to understand literature, to be a successful test taker, and to feel proud of your command of the English language. Writing will be incorporated into the vocabulary program, allowing for reinforcement and application of new words.

Often learners want to go at their own pace. This year you will be able to build your own lexicon at a speed that provides options. As you know, many people have a say in your education, so please read each of the options available with a family member and decide what your goals are as a team by focusing on what is best for you and your learning for this trimester.

You will receive four one hundred point test grades for your commitment to vocabulary this trimester based upon the sliding scale below. You will still earn the grade of each of the tests, quizzes, and writing assignments that you complete this trimester. It is the average of these four test scores and the tests, quizzes, and writing that will make up your total vocabulary development grade.

GRADE   EXPLANATION

75% C   Complete three vocabulary units[1] by November 2nd and complete one writing assignment[2] utilizing ten vocabulary words[3] by September 21st (three quizzes, one test, and one writing assignment total).

80% B–   Complete four vocabulary units by November 2nd and complete one writing assignment utilizing ten vocabulary words by September 21st (four quizzes, one test, and one writing assignment total).

85% B   Complete four vocabulary units by November 2nd. Complete two writing assignments utilizing ten vocabulary words in each: one by September 21st and the other by October 5th (four quizzes, one test, and two writing assignments total).

90% A–   Complete five vocabulary units by November 2nd. Complete two writing assignments utilizing ten vocabulary words in each: one by September 21st and the other by October 5th (five quizzes, one test, and two writing assignments total).

95% A   Complete five vocabulary units by November 2nd. Complete three writing assignments utilizing ten vocabulary words in each: one by September 21st, one by October 5th, and the last by October 19th (five quizzes, one test, and three writing assignments total).

100% A+   Complete five vocabulary units by November 2nd. Complete four writing assignments utilizing ten vocabulary words in each: one by September 21st, one by October 5th, one by October 19th, and the last by October 26th (five quizzes, one test, and four writing assignments total).

---

1. Complete Vocabulary Units = Complete each exercise in the vocabulary textbook as well as one set of vocabulary cards. Cards are completed as a learning tool for retention.
2. Complete one writing assignment = This writing assignment may be any writing assignment you have this trimester in any class. You must turn this assignment in by the due date and receive an 85% on the assignment by November 2, 2001.
3. Utilizing ten vocabulary words = These words must be used correctly and show that you thoroughly understand their meaning. Context clues are a must.

FIGURE 3–1. *Vocabulary Contract for Eighth Grade*

I have spoken to those most important to me about my vocabulary grade for the trimester. Below is the agreement that we have decided is reasonable and one in which I will, with all good intent, attain.

Vocabulary Text, Quizzes, and Tests
The vocabulary text will be checked on each Tuesday and Thursday of the trimester starting on August 30th. Vocabulary Quizzes and Tests may be taken on these dates as the students become ready for them. These dates are outlined below:

August 30
September 4, 6, 11, 13, 18, 20, 25, 27
October 2, 4, 9, 11, 16, 18, 23, 25, 30
November 1, 6

Vocabulary Cards must include the word and pronunciation on the blank side and all definitions and the parts of speech on the lined side. I know that on ten of the cards of my own choosing I will place a picture to help me solidify my understanding. I realize that only neat cards will be accepted as completed.

Example:

Word	*(Part of Speech) All Definitions*
Breach	**(n) an opening, gap; a violation**
(Pronunciation)	**or infraction**
(brēch)	**(v) to create an opening, break**
A picture without words should be added here for emphasis	**through**

I will aspire to get a _____% this trimester. I know of the requirements for such a grade and will work to the best of my ability to reach that goal. I know that I must earn at least a 90% on each requirement of this grade to earn credit for that requirement to be considered completed.

Student:
Printed Name _____

Signature _____

Parent:
Printed Name _____

Signature _____

FIGURE 3–1. *continued*

vocabulary development for that marking period, then the student, parent, and teacher would all understand what the requirements were before the job was begun.

This contract also allowed me to individualize instruction for those students who needed more time with the information. Though the contract and its requirements were written for the majority of the class, it did give me the flexibility to say to a student and her parents, "Gloria can earn an A in vocabulary development this marking period if she completes all of the requirements for a C on this contract." No student knows what any other student is trying to earn, for all students need to concentrate only on their own goals. This anonymity is just one of the positive aspects of this contract.

To make sure that the contract went smoothly, I needed systems in place for the students to check their workbooks, check their vocabulary cards, have time to study, have a quiet place to take tests or write, and receive timely information back about individual progress. This required me to set certain dates of the trimester aside as quizzing and testing dates and to plan deadlines for all written work.

After experiencing the regimented plan in which everyone took the same quiz on the same day, students were excited about being given the opportunity to learn at their own pace. They appreciated being treated like adults in that they had been given a *job to do*. That job had to be completed by a certain date, and if they completed the job, they earned the payment, or grade, that they wanted.

The students that I knew would flourish did so. They worked ahead at home and completed quizzes and tests early. They took each quiz and test once, gaining a 90 percent or higher every time, and their writing samples were exquisite.

There were many students that appreciated knowing the requirements of the contract ahead of time. They knew what to expect and what needed to be accomplished to earn the grade. They took quizzes and tests as well as turned in writing samples on time. Some had to take some tests or quizzes over again to master the information, but overall these students were the solid base of each class.

There were, of course, those students who did self-destruct; they began with great intentions, but the battle for their attention was won by other distractions. Time was always an issue with these students, and studying for the quiz or test the night before or on the last day possible was a frequent habit. These students packed in a large amount of information in a very short time, barely meeting deadlines and sometimes missing their original goals because there just wasn't any more time left to rewrite assigned writings or to retake quizzes or tests.

Then there were those that just never got into the contract at all. I called their parents and held conferences. Some did the minimum and some did not.

Overall, even though there was considerable work up front on my part to make the schedule, create the systems for students to take the quizzes and tests, and grade all of it so that students were aware of their progress, I am pleased with the results of the contract system. Students had ultimate control over their learning, and class vocabulary averages from earlier in the year increased by more than 15 percent.

How to Make It Happen

1. Whatever vocabulary program is used, teachers must first look at their time frame so that they can make decisions about the requirements for each letter grade. This includes how much information is to be processed, quizzed, and tested. The more work completed, the higher grade that student should earn.
2. Next the teacher must prepare a contract that outlines all of the requirements. Students need detailed time frames or deadlines, writing assignment requirements, testing and quizzing dates, and any specific assignments like workbook exercises and vocabulary flash cards. The more information, the clearer the contract. See Figure 3–1.
3. Teachers need to make all copies of tests and quizzes and set up the room to maximize student learning before the contract begins. Teachers might also want to make posters that list quiz and test dates or specific contract requirements that students may need to see often. Just having a copy of the contract is not always enough.
4. Teachers need to go over expectations often. The more students hear them, or see them on the posters mentioned previously, the more they will take responsibility for this requirement.
5. During the testing and quizzing days, teachers should take time to meet with students to check on their progress by checking on their workbooks or just asking the students what they are working on that day. Record keeping is important to the success of the contract, and the more that is done as the marking period continues, the easier it is to maintain. Teachers should contact parents if for any reason their child is falling behind. Parents will know about the contract because they will have read and signed it before the contract period began.

Like Reading Contracts (see Chapter 2), Vocabulary Contracts offer students the ability to choose their grade as well as require them to involve their parents and teacher in educational decisions. Vocabulary Contracts allow students to have a voice in choosing the amount and type of work that suits them, and this provides them with an aspect of control over a part of the English curriculum that they usually have little power over.

Adaptations

- Differentiated Instruction: In the How to Make It Happen section, we said, "The more work completed, the higher grade that the student should earn." This is usually true, but individual students learn and process at different rates. With this in mind, teachers could individualize these contracts even more by allowing a student who can obviously find success within this system but cannot possibly handle the volume that the rest of the class can handle to still earn a high grade. Creating individual goals will let that student work within the systems that are in place but with realistic expectations. A B for one student might be an A+ for another.

- A Vocabulary Contract can work with vocabulary garnered completely from the students' outside reading. The procedures that are put in place could be basically the same as those of a *program* but without the tests and quizzes. If written expression is more important to teachers or their administrations, students could have a Vocabulary Contract based solely upon the written work that the students turn in that proves that they have learned certain words from their reading and writing.

- Teachers could assign words that are known to be useful to a certain group. The contract could require students to show how they utilize these words in conversation as well as in their written expression.

- Any student who finds any of the vocabulary words in print could earn extra credit by bringing in that piece of writing.

- Extra credit could be given to any student who brings in a vocabulary word that has been utilized incorrectly or spelled wrong.

- Many ESE students have vocabulary goals as a part of their individual education plan (IEP). It is important that their mastery goal for the Vocabulary Contract and their mastery goal for their IEP are the same percentage. The Vocabulary Contract is an excellent way to have students prove mastery and help with an ESE teacher's paper trail.

Q & A

What if students sign up to earn a B but do only enough work to earn a C?

Communication among all the stakeholders is in order. Long before the contract period is up, parents should be informed that their child is falling behind the expectations set by the contract, which could state that whatever requirements are completed by the end date will garner that particular grade. If teachers have done all that can be done to help students achieve their initial goal, and students still decide that they have done enough, then they should receive the lesser grade. As long as the teacher, the student, and the parent are aware of what grade will be earned based upon the student's effort, then the child has truly earned that grade.

What if students supercede their own expectations and do more than they signed up for ten weeks earlier?

Teachers should celebrate it and parade the students around (even if only by writing a note to their parents explaining their achievement). If students do the work for a higher grade, then they have earned it! Students should feel the responsibility for the commitment of the contract from the beginning, but they should also know that it is possible to go beyond their original goal. Setting long-term goals and achieving them is one of the life lessons that this contract can teach. More power to those students who originally aimed for a B but then earned an A.

What if students do less than the minimum by not fulfilling even the lowest of expectations?

This is handled on a case-by-case basis. Students see the power of their own choices. If it is possible to involve parents and also the administration, that may be an option. Students should be given every opportunity to improve their work and their grade, but ultimately, the grade earned should equal the work completed.

What if parents force their child to try to earn a grade higher than the child can possibly attain?

Parents are important players in this process, and many different scenarios could occur. Students could be fueled to do better than anyone thought they could and succeed. Students could perform as they themselves thought they would, which is lower than their parents wanted, and communication could begin. Lastly, there is the extreme example where students completely shut down in defiance because of all of the pressure, all but securing a lower grade than they should have attained, at which time it may be necessary to contact a parent to alleviate this problem in future contracts. All of these are possible scenarios, but all of them have an outcome that promotes talk about education between parents and their children. Having these conversations is important, and the teacher is simply the one who sets the stage, suggests improvements, provides encouragement, and even holds some hands. But once the contract begins, it is up to the students and their parents to decide what happens next.

Visual Vocabulary Quiz

As a new teacher, Terry struggled with the idea of teaching and testing vocabulary. In his first teaching assignment in a major metropolitan southeastern city, the curriculum was scripted and students and teachers had few choices. Teachers were provided with the list of words they would use, told how they would use them, and *encouraged* to use a standard vocabulary matching and fill-in-type test to assess mastery of the week's vocabulary.

Struggling with ways to get his students to learn vocabulary in this scenario, Terry and a colleague discovered what was probably not a new idea, but a good one: the Visual Vocabulary Quiz.

Visual Vocabulary Quizzes allow students to learn vocabulary from a text that they read as a class but to find a way to express knowledge of the word that suits them. It offers a choice between responding to a word with a definition, a sentence with the word used in context, or a graphic image. It also allows students a chance to get feedback from their peers before the quiz begins. The point is for the students to own the words, not to *get students* when they don't. Thus, Visual Vocabulary Quizzes were created.

Terry's Experience

Upon returning to Tampa for my second year of teaching, I knew that vocabulary was going to be important at my new school, but I also knew the administration would allow me to do what I thought was best for my students. I wanted students' vocabulary words to come from their reading, not an arbitrary list that would have no meaning for them.

I began reading ahead in works that we would use in class and compiling words that might be appropriate for my particular students. I had one advanced group and another regular group that included about ten mainstreamed exceptional students. I decided I would choose the same words for each group and see what happened. Each week, the students received the words, looked them up, and then took the test by defining the words on a piece of notebook paper. I ran into the same problem with both groups: they could not remember the definitions very well, but when I spoke with them after the quiz, they would often be able to use and describe most of the words perfectly. I was extremely frustrated.

I decided to find a way to approach vocabulary that would allow students to show that they knew the words even if they couldn't remember the exact definitions. A conversation with a colleague helped me come to the conclusion that I wanted my students to own the words, not to just be tested and then forget them. I decided what owning a word meant to me and I came up with the following: knowing how to use the word, being able to use it in discussion and conversation, and using it in their writing showed that students owned a word. I also decided that students didn't have to learn ten words each week. If there were not ten words worth learning, then six would be OK. If there were twelve that were really worthwhile another week, so be it.

I decided that students could show they were on the road to word ownership through several types of response. One was writing the definition or using the word in a sentence with context clues to show they knew the word. A new twist was to draw a picture showing the word in action, or they could show a piece of writing they were working on that included the word used properly.

I thought I had a winner.

The first time I used this as a vocabulary quiz, I saw hope, but it still needed some fine-tuning. I told students that they would be able to draw the words if they liked, and when the test day came, they did. Most of their pictures just didn't show the meaning of the words clearly. Again I returned to my original premise: I just wanted students to learn and own words.

At the start of the next week, I gave students the words for the week on Monday along with the page numbers of the stories in which they appeared. I placed baskets of highlighters in the middle of the tables and encouraged students to highlight the words on the handouts and in the books as we came across them. This was traumatic for some students, as they had never been allowed to write in or mark up a book and now they were being encouraged to commit this heinous crime! Each day, I gave students time to figure out their own definition for each word encountered that day from context, draw a picture to represent it, and write an original sentence with that word used properly. The next step was the most important.

Next they were to examine each other's work to make sure that they all knew the words. This social interaction was important because the kids gave each other feedback and readjusted their various definitions in response to this feedback. The discussion of the words was a thrill to observe:

"You can't just show a nose for *inhaled*, you've got to show air and stuff going in!"

This feedback is where learning happens. When students negotiate and renegotiate the meaning of words, arguing about their meaning and discussing how best to portray that meaning, students begin to own the words. Is this process time-consuming? Certainly. If the goal is for students to add the words to their working vocabulary, does it work? Definitely.

This approach to vocabulary is successful because it allows students to discuss language, show what they know in a variety of ways, and use vocabulary from the texts they are reading.

How to Make It Happen

The most difficult part of making this approach work is preparing the words in advance. Because of their teaching situation (many preparations, new curriculum, new grade level or school), some teachers barely have time to read and prepare lessons, let alone look for appropriate words to use for vocabulary in the next week's reading. If teachers have time to do this, however, Visual Vocabulary Quizzes are an effective way to get students to learn and own new words.

1. Teachers should choose the six to fifteen words they plan to use each week. This will vary with the ability and age of their students. High school seniors can certainly be expected to carry a heavier load than third graders, but the words should always be worth knowing.

2. Have students divide their paper into quarters by folding it in half and in half again. This will give them four boxes on the front and back of their paper to make notes, drawings, and so on for each word. Give them the words and the page numbers where the words will appear in their reading for the week. This will allow students to look for the words as they are reading and highlight or underline them in pencil if appropriate. They can then return to these words in context quickly to refresh their memory of their meaning. If you want to save the time it takes for students to create their own sheets and record the words and page numbers, you can provide students with a handout with the boxes and words already filled in.

3. Provide time each day, at the end of class or the beginning of the next class, for students to write a personal definition, create an original sen-

tence, and draw a graphic for each word encountered that day. This can be done for homework if students are allowed to take the text home with them.

4. The next step is the most critical stage if words are to be owned by the students. Teachers must provide time for students to give feedback to each other about the definitions, sentences, and drawings they have created. This is the step where learning happens. Students will negotiate meaning and make adjustments to their work. This can be time-consuming, but when students argue about the meaning of a word and return to the text to support their answer, learning is happening.

5. At an appropriate time, students will know there will be a vocabulary quiz. Provide the blank grid with the words and allow students to respond with their definition, an original sentence, or a drawing to show they know the word. If they have gone through this process, they should do well on the quizzes and teachers should see and hear the words begin popping up in class writing and discussions.

Students are provided with choice in this assignment in that they are given the words, but they create the definitions, sentences, and drawings to support each word. On their quiz, students decide how they can best depict their knowledge of the words. Students will almost always choose the method that best suits them and provides them with the best chance to succeed.

Adaptations

- Differentiated Instruction: Adjust the number and difficulty of words for the audience. This seems like a simple thing, but it took Terry a while to understand that it didn't matter if students learned twenty, ten, or five words each week as long as they learned them well and in context.

- Allow students to choose a number of the words from the text. The teacher might provide five of the words and let students provide three more of their own choosing. Some discussion of how to choose these words is important, but this provides students with more choice and control over what they are learning.

- Use the idea of learning vocabulary with independent reading. Teachers can have students choose five words per week from their individual reading to include in their vocabulary quiz.

- Teachers can require that a portion of the words come from environmental reading, that is, print they encounter out in the world.

Students may have to choose one word they encountered out in the community (e.g., on a billboard) to include in their vocabulary words for the week.

- Teachers may choose to use this approach in conjunction with the Reading Memo format (see Chapter 2).
- Interdisciplinary Instruction: Teachers may require that students choose a word or two from science or history classes, or teachers could work together so that the requirements for one assignment are checked in both classes for credit.

Q & A

How much time does this take?

This approach can take a great deal of time when teachers first begin to include it in their practice. Once students become accustomed to the procedure, it becomes pretty painless. It will take a little longer to get through texts, but the learning will be richer in the end and the students' use of language will be noticeably improved.

What if students still aren't getting it?

Some students may need to start with fewer words or be allowed to respond in ways that use a multisensory approach. Students need to be challenged to expand their vision of the words by being able to own them in various ways.

4

Choice in Writing

When involved, the writer made the task his own and began to write to satisfy himself as well as his teacher . . .

—James Britton

One of the most difficult communication skills to acquire is proficiency in writing. One reason is simply that the writer is never done. Ever. Every piece of writing can always be changed, edited, revised, or improved. We have revised, and edited this page alone a dozen times. Hemingway, moreover, reportedly rewrote the ending to *Old Man and the Sea* more than eighty times before it was published. How can we as teachers ever hope to become experts at writing or hope that our students will want to go beyond their first draft when a master like Hemingway has difficulty satisfying even himself?

One way is through practice. We, as teachers of writing, try to offer our students numerous opportunities to write that are varied in scope and genre in the hope that they will continue to grow into the writing process that they have learned from their first days of school. We do this through short pieces of writing that focus on particular skills and try to make students aware of the choices that are available to them as writers as well as provide opportunities to write on a larger scale, having students apply their cumulative knowledge and writing skills. In the pages that follow, teachers will find activities to use at varying points in the teaching of the writing process.

The start of the year poses particular problems in getting students to produce their initial pieces of writing. Many students say, "I don't know what to write about. Nothing ever happens to me." They truthfully believe they have nothing to say. In this case, the Life Map guides students in finding specific events in their lives that are worth writing about and culminates in at least one piece of personal experience writing.

Later in the year, students may be asked to reflect on what they have learned by producing Portfolio Write-Ups. These reflections provide students a chance to examine what they have done, what they can do now that they couldn't do before, and what they want to accomplish in the future. It allows students to reflect on themselves as students and praise themselves for a job well done and also allows for some brainstorming about how they might improve. This kind of introspective self-examination leads to the best kind of learning.

Immediately after we have taught our students how to write one way, we might have to shift gears to teach another. There are so many writing skills as well as so many possible ways to present these options to students. Sometimes, we have a hard time deciding on the best method to teach any one writing skill or style, so the Definition Approach is a reminder that sometimes great answers can be found when we come back to sqaure one.

Teachers often create specific writing assignments to allow students to show that they have acquired and can use particular skills. The Scriptwriting project found in this chapter can help students focus on character, setting, and dialogue—three of the most difficult skills to teach new writers.

Finally, as teachers we sometimes want to teach our students long-range goal setting within the framework of our classrooms. The Chapbook project at the end of this chapter asks students to work on a yearlong project incorporating reading, writing in several genres, interviewing, and producing several types of artwork. It requires that students look ahead to due dates and plan carefully how to use their time in the context of a massive language arts project based upon an individualized, student-chosen topic.

Writing is a huge part of what we do as English teachers. It is also a critical life skill for our students, and we hope that these activities add to the many varied ways you already teach your students.

Life Map

Write about what you know. —Mark Twain

Personal experience writing is one of the most important kinds of writing with which a developing author can experiment because young people often feel like they are not good at anything, when, in fact, they are the leading authority on themselves, their age group, and their environment. One of the struggles that teachers have when they ask students to write about their personal experiences is this reply: "Nothing ever happens to me!" Students feel that their lives are boring and they cannot wait to race into adulthood where life is bound to be exciting.

We found inspiration for solving the adolescent personal writing *blahs* in Linda Rief's *Seeking Diversity* (1992). Rief developed Positive-Negative Graphs, which require students to create a visual representation of the important events in their lives. The Life Map is an adaptation of Rief's idea and has inspired some fantastic personal experience writing from students.

Terry's Experience

Greg began eighth grade in neutral, and over the first few weeks of school, he seemed to have little intention of ever putting himself in gear. This is not an unusual behavior to see from middle school boys, but Greg was different. I was uneasy right from the moment I met him.

When asked, even the most reluctant young man will give me at least a halfhearted effort in reply, but not Greg. I held him after class numerous times to see if I could plead, beg, negotiate, threaten, or cajole him into doing something for my class, all to no avail.

When the third week began, I introduced Life Maps to my class. We discussed topics on which the students were the experts, and I then had them go through the process outlined here to create their own Life Map. As we went, I modeled each step to ensure that all students would be successful. All the while, Greg was completing a Life Map right beneath my nose.

When the due date arrived at the end of the week, I walked around and collected all student Life Maps while the students were engaged in writing a short personal experience piece based on one event on their Life Map. I didn't even stop at Greg's desk because I assumed that the papers he had out were doodles or some such thing.

"Hey, Bigelow," I heard from behind me, "don'tcha want mine?"

When I turned around, Greg casually handed me his Life Map as if this were another in a long line of assignments he had already turned in. I stood with my mouth agape. I looked at the paper, and sure enough, it was titled, "Greg's Life Map."

"Uh, yeah. Thanks," I stammered. I finished collecting the maps and went to set them on my desk. Once there, I acted like I was working on my piece of writing, but really I was spying. I was looking for some evidence that this new Greg was a doppelganger of some kind; an alien shape changer that had plans of taking over the world one eighth-grade classroom at a time. But it was Greg, and he was actually writing a personal experience piece!

At the end of class, students turned in the beginnings of this writing as an exit ticket, and again I was floored when Greg dropped his writing into my hands. "Thank you," I choked, stunned.

Eventually, Greg did put himself in gear, but only sporadically. He often spent a great deal of time coasting, too. The victory was getting him to have that first taste of success in my class. Beyond that, he would choose what he would try and what he wouldn't.

After that first assignment he turned in, I never assumed that the papers on his desk were anything but his assignment ready to turn in. This reminded me that any assignment that is engaging might be the one to kick-start a reluctant student or put a student who is doing mediocre work into high gear.

How to Make It Happen

Life Maps are simple to do, but they can take longer for students to complete than first expected. Some of them will struggle with the idea of *events that have happened to them* and they will need a teacher to model this entire process as he goes through the directions. To make the Life Map happen, the following steps will be helpful:

1. The teacher should list the ten best and ten worst things that have ever happened to him. It will be very helpful if the teacher gives personal examples of both of these and creates his own list for the students to see. Terry uses the example of a broken arm in 1977 that was the result of falling out of a tree that his father had specifically told him not to climb. This first step might take an entire class period for students to complete.
2. Next, students should circle, star, or somehow indicate the five most memorable events from the good list and the bad list. These are the ten events they will work with to create their Life Map.
3. Once students have made these decisions, they should try to figure out when these events happened. They can tell what age they were (age nine), what year it was (1996), or even give an exact date (March 17, 2003) if the event is that memorable. The point is to state when each thing happened in relation to the other events on the list.
4. Next, students create a new list with all ten of these events, both best and worst, in time order, like a time line. Students often want to create a *good* list and a *bad* list, but it is critical that they understand that all events will appear on the same list, starting with when they were born and ending on the date the Life Map is due. Often, if students are asked to put *born* as number one and *due date* as number twelve, they comprehend what they are expected to do in between.
5. Next, teachers should ask students to draw or find a graphic to represent each of the ten events. In Terry's experience, many students feel like they can't draw, so he reassures them that they will not be judged

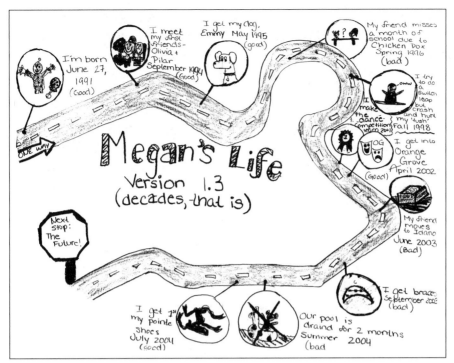

Within the image:
I meet my first friends- Olivia + Pilar September 1994 (Good)

I get my dog, Emmy May 1995 (good)

My friend misses a month of school due to Chicken Pox Spring 1996 (bad)

I'm born June 27, 1991 (Good)

Megan's Life
Version 1.3
(decades, that is)

I try to do a switch leap but crash and hurt my 'tush' Fall 1998

I make the dance competition team 2001

I get into Orange Grove April 2002 (Good)

ONE WAY

Next Stop: The Future!

My friend moves to Idaho June 2003 (Bad)

I get 1st my pointe shoes July 2004 (Good)

Our pool is drained for 2 months Summer 2004 (bad

I get braces September 2002 (bad)

FIGURE 4–1. *Meagan's Life Map*

on their artistic ability but instead on the time, effort, energy, and care they put into the job.

6. When the previous steps are completed, teachers should give students some high-quality drawing paper if available. This sends a message to students that the important events in their lives are too important to drawn on regular copy or notebook paper. This may inspire them to put even more care into the final product. See Figure 4–1.

7. Finally, students should be provided the criteria for grading. They need to be told what is expected of them in the final copy of their Life Map. Terry creates a simple rubric that guides students in the number of life events that should be included in their final Life Map, how colorful it should be, how neat it should be, and if it should have a title or not. Each teacher can decide what criteria are important to her or him while still allowing students plenty of ownership in the assignment.

Students love most assignments that put them in the spotlight. This assignment is all about them. It makes them realize that *stuff* does happen to them and that it might even be worth writing about. The final step in this assignment is to choose one of these memorable events to write about. An effective way to do this is for the teacher to share a personal experience piece of her own about one of the events the teacher offered as an example for her Life Map.

Teachers should prepare and copy or read aloud a sample piece of writing that is directly about one of the items on their Life Map. Next, teachers should share this with students so they can see the gravity of a situation or the humor in looking back at something their teachers did in their youth. Finally, teachers can have students determine what makes the writing good and what makes it work and then ask them to make it happen with their own writing.

Adaptations

- Of course, depending on the time available to spend on this activity, the teacher may change the number of events that students are expected to work with as they create a final copy of their Life Map.
- Teachers may use the Life Map to show the progression of another person's life studied from a biography or an autobiography.
- After reading a book, a student could create a Life Map about a character from the book.
- Students also can create a Life Map for several characters in a book and have the lines overlap and intersect. The connections can be graphically designed to reveal the nature of the interaction (e.g., if the characters fought, then the line may be jagged, and broken; if characters fell in love, then the lines may be soft and curvy).
- As with Linda Rief's Positive-Negative Graph, a student can go to this wellspring of personal ideas for writing, and the teacher may require the student to write several types of writing from these events.
- Students could interview their parents or family members and create a Life Map of an important person in their family. The next step would be to write a story based on one of the events in the family member's life.
- Differentiated Instruction: Visuals of the teacher's example are essential for understanding of the chronological aspect of the Life Map.
- Interdisciplinary Instruction: Life Maps are a good way to show the ups and downs of anyone's life. This assignment can be adapted for figures studied in other disciplines.

Q & A

How long should a teacher be expected to spend on this project?

This is a time-consuming project for students. In Terry's experience, students often have difficulty generating the original list of ten good and ten bad events that have happened to them. The other part of this project that is time-consuming for students is determining when each event happened to them. The rest of the Life Map usually goes pretty quickly, though they will need at least one or two forty-five-minute periods in class and then time outside of class just to create the final copy.

Further Resources

Golub, Jeffrey N. 1994. *Activities for an Interactive Classroom*. Urbana, IL: National Council of Teachers of English.

Rief, Linda. 1992. *Seeking Diversity*. Portsmouth, NH: Heinemann.

Portfolio Write-Up

There are many fads in the world of education that are presented as cure-alls. New ways to write, read, spell, or even schedule the days have been implemented and rescinded like the ebb and flow of the tide. Monumental, classroom-changing ideas have been forced down teachers' throats with a smile and a "We don't know if this will work, but it seems like a good idea. Go make it work in your classroom and tell us if we are right."

From the moment Michael heard about portfolios, he believed that they were just another educational trend, but when his school adopted a policy of using portfolios that travel with students from the primary grades through the eighth grade, he was forced to look at the portfolio more closely. He came to realize the possibilities for introspection that portfolios and their accompanying write-ups allow for students. Eventually, the Portfolio Write-Up became an assignment worth doing, but it took some time to work out the kinks.

Michael's Experience

I will admit that because of stubbornness and an aversion to fads, I usually resist what I hear is the latest wave in education. I think I get this cynical view from undergoing the complete mess that was *new math* back when I was in junior high. Now that I am an educator, I really think it is important for me to look at ideas from the students' perspective. Is this really necessary? Will this skill help them? Why do it at all?

When I first heard of portfolios, I was immediately skeptical because the sum total of what a colleague had learned in a workshop about portfolios was compiling information in a binder and decorating it. But this fad didn't go away. More and more colleagues began to use them. My school even spoke about compiling work from a student and then having the portfolio follow the student from grade to grade to give a complete picture of the growth and maturity of that student, but I continued to resist.

Then portfolios became a requirement. They were coming to my eighth-grade English class whether I liked it or not, so I had a reason to find a way to make them worthwhile. I forced myself to look at the portfolio from the student's point of view and create an assignment that was worth doing. I can look back now and appreciate the opportunity I had been given because this assignment became one that not only allowed students to look at their progress but also allowed them a level of introspection that had been missing in my class.

With all of this said, I decided to require students to reflect on themselves using each of the seven major areas upon which my classroom focused: reading, writing, grammar, vocabulary, speaking, listening, and viewing. I asked students to find one *artifact* per area that represented them and their work over the past twelve weeks. This artifact could be a copy of a quiz, an essay, a test, a book cover, a vocabulary card, or a picture of a scary cat. Students could choose any object that fit on an $8^1/_2$-by-11-inch piece of paper as long as they could support their reasoning for choosing that artifact. I then asked them to answer two questions for each artifact:

1. Why did you choose this artifact over any other?
2. What does this artifact say about you as an English student?

The first question encouraged students to choose more than just their best work. I found that when I prompted students to speak to not only the positives but the negatives of their experiences as English students, I could cultivate a richer crop of reflections.

The second question allowed students to share their personal thoughts about each area of English. Through the Portfolio Write-Ups, I found that I had Regina all wrong, for example. I thought that she hated to read and loved to write because all I had ever seen in class was someone who constantly *forgot* her book at home but someone who also turned in solid work for each writing assignment. Regina shared through the portfolio write-ups that she instead loved to read and hated to write.

The reality of the situation was that Regina left her book at home because she didn't want to look like a show-off to her classmates. Because of her appetite for books, Regina read at least a book a week, and she shared that it was safer to just act dumb than be ridiculed by her peers. At the same time, she had to work very hard to create the writing that she produced. Even though she had done well on each writing assignment, the only way she did so was by working diligently, writing rough draft after rough draft to ultimately create her final drafts. Each assignment appeared effortless to me as the teacher, but to Regina, each was a chore. The Portfolio Write-Up allowed Regina to have a safe place to share the underlying reality of what was happening at school and at home. It allowed the student to make a deep connection with herself as well as with me. I found a Regina that I hadn't realized existed.

However, as with any instruction, the assignment was not immediately successful, and I received Portfolio Write-Ups like the following, which Cathy wrote:

GRAMMAR

I chose this for my grammar section because it took time and thought to write this ABR [*Alternative Book Report*] and my grade reflects the time that I put in. We had to compare literature to a mirror or a window. I think that it is really has nothing to do with literature but oh well. I think this piece reflects me as a student because it's good.

And John wrote:

VOCABULARY

The Unit 7 vocabulary quiz is on my portfolio because even though I could have done better had I studied, I got an above average grade with no preparation. That reflects exactly how most all of my vocabulary quizzes have been because memorizing things comes naturally to me. I have always done well especially in vocabulary because it is just being fed information and spitting it back out.

I received write-ups like these at first because I gave the students only the two questions without guidance. I wanted to see what they would create without a model, and I got precisely what I deserved. If I wanted deep introspection, I would need to guide them there. They needed a map.

I decided to teach students about metacognition, the awareness and understanding of one's own thinking, through examples and nonexamples. Students in middle school don't often think about their own thinking. They take almost everything at face value. Their thinking is as follows: My teacher gives an assignment, and I do it because I want a good grade or because my parents will kill me if I don't or because that is what I think I am supposed to do.

I needed to educate my students about why they take a class for twelve years in their native language. I needed to explain why we read literature, study vocabulary, grapple with grammar, become succinct with speech, and write, write, and rewrite. In my experience, my students have been in school without understanding the *why*. They *do* because they always have *done*, so when I required them to answer these introspective questions, I got back exactly what they had been fed: "I do because I am told to," or "I do because I am good at it," or "I do but I stink at it."

I ended up educating my students on the *why* by having discussions about education that included why we read literature, study vocabulary, and even see the same concept many times year after year. After we had this kind of educational *what for* seminar, I challenged them to look into themselves to see how they were doing. I asked, "Are you putting the effort into the assignments you need to reach your goals? Do you have any goals? What does a ninety-seven out of one hundred on a test really say about your study habits? Does this come easily to you, or are you clawing and scratching just to make a C? Why?" I dared students to find flaws in anything we did in class. I wanted to know what they thought of the assignments that I gave, and I sought after suggestions for tweaking or completely changing any assignment for the better.

With a room full of challenged and informed students, I eventually began to get deeper reflection on the *why* behind their assignments as well as themselves. As it turned out, I learned more about my students both as learners and as individuals.

Mary wrote:

EIGHTH GRADE—THIRD TRIMESTER—SPEAKING

From all the areas of English, Speaking is my favorite. Every assignment that pertains to Speaking I truly enjoy. I feel very comfortable with speaking "projects" because I get so much practice from numerous school and religious events. This artifact displays my "project" for Poetry Coffee House. This was a unique project grading my poetry presentation and "presentation skills." I am so proud of the A+ I received from my performance. My mom was my audience, so I practiced several times until it was perfect. Mr. Vokoun brainstormed ideas to enhance my presentation. It really helped knowing who my audience was. I knew where to take my poem. I put projection, motion, and emotion to bring my poem and presentation to life.

In the past, in this area and in Poetry Coffee House I haven't had any trouble. The effort I put into this performance says I always put my heart into everything I do. I love all [of] the assignment and put forth so much quality into it. The only part I need to improve on is using my space better on stage. I tend to usually stand in one place. Otherwise, I will continue to work hard and succeed.

How to Make It Happen

1. Teachers must create the framework upon which students will hang their reflections. Michael utilized the seven major areas of English (reading, writing, grammar, vocabulary, speaking, listening, and viewing), but other teachers might want a different framework or choose to focus on particular areas at different times of the year.

2. Teachers should give students the explanation as to *why* they are taking this class (or let them develop it; see Adaptations), for with this deeper understanding that education is something that they can take advantage of and have full control of instead of something that is done to them, their reflections will take on more meaning. It is easy to assume that students know why taking English is important. Considering this question was an important step in increasing student metacognition and the chance for true introspection in Michael's class. It was the difference between the wooden fill-in-the-blank assignment and the assignment that lived for each child.

3. Teachers should give students the questions that they should answer. Teachers may have more direct questions than the ones posed earlier. Ability, personality, and willingness of certain classes can have a particular effect upon what questions the teacher wants to have them answer.

4. Teachers should then educate the students on the type of response that would be most beneficial to them. Examples and nonexamples work best to bring a point home. Thinking about why they were successful (or not) and what they learned from each assignment allows students to place the responsibility for their learning square upon the shoulders of the people most in charge of it—themselves. If it is clear to students what type of response will be accepted, teachers might be spared those dry write-ups.

5. For best results, teachers should try to do this assignment more than once a year. Students change as the year progresses, and allowing a safe place where the students can stop and think three or more times a year can allow them, as well as their parents and their teacher, to track their progress.

Portfolio Write-Ups allow students to select the work that best represents how they have grown as students in English/language arts. This selection process allows students to choose what they think is their best work and describe it in the light they see fit. It also makes students reflect and empowers them in the process of proving their newly honed or learned talents.

Adaptations

- Portfolios can be made for just one area of a class. If reading is a major focus for a class, a reading portfolio that is updated frequently may shed some light on individual student progress as well as reveal any difficulties that the students are having during the process.
- Portfolios could be done as a year-end assignment that requires students to find many pieces within each area to show their progress and impediments throughout the year.
- Portfolios could be done completely electronically. Instead of a binder to put on a shelf, the students could create an interactive portfolio that includes assignments, quizzes, and even movies of poetry performances at the school's Poetry Coffeehouse (discussed in Chapter 5).
- Portfolio questions could require students to look into their future to see how assignments that are completed today could help them with future endeavors.
- The portfolio binder itself can be unwieldy. The binder or folder, many dividers, the artifacts, and the write-ups all need to be combined into a final product. There are many different variations in what that product can look like. If students create the binder to the teacher's specifications and then also turn in the write-ups separately, their teacher will have all of the write-ups in one place, and the grading process becomes much easier by eliminating flipping through and marking write-ups within a portfolio. Corrected versions should then be placed behind the originals within the portfolio so that students and parents can see both what is finalized and what is in process.
- Another grading tip is to tell the students that the teacher will be grading only one write-up and that the teacher will choose that area of class (grammar, for instance) on the day the students turn in the work. This encourages students to work hard on their entire collection of write-ups, and it cuts down on the teacher's workload significantly.
- The portfolio and its write-ups could be the centerpiece of a student-parent-teacher conference. The student leads the conference, taking her parents through the portfolio. By reading the write-ups and showing the specific artifacts, the student shows her progress as an English student throughout the year. If this is done toward the end of the year,

especially after the students have completed the same assignment three or four times, parents will be able to get an accurate portrayal of their child's growth and areas of refinement over an extended time period.

- This assignment could become an Alternative Book Report (described in Chapter 2). The student would choose a character and create the portfolio as if he were that character. The students could choose those items that would tell the most about the character and the story itself with these artifacts, and questions could change to What does this artifact say about you as a strong father, good brother, best friend, morally imperfect person? Possibilities abound.

- Interdisciplinary Instruction: This option can work across all disciplines. Teachers could have the students discuss the *why* of a class instead of just handing them a syllabus, curriculum, class expectations sheet, or our personal opinions. With a little guidance, students can be given the opportunity to work in groups and create a short answer to the prompt Why do we take English for twelve years? or generate a list of reasons that social studies is an important subject. Some deep conversations can spark students to understand why they take a class in the first place as well as to realize the power that they have within themselves as students and as learners.

Q & A

What if students continue to turn in those blah *write-ups?*

Depending upon the philosophy and workload of the teacher, having the students keep working on their write-ups until they produce something valuable is an option. The philosophy of Michael's school is to give students the ability to redo an assignment until they master the content. However, introspection is a mater of maturity, so forcing maturity on a student can be tricky at best. Teachers need to use their best judgment when deciding whether to have a student redo this assignment.

Further Resources

Mahoney, Jim. 2002. *Power and Portfolios: Best Practices for High School Classrooms.* Portsmouth, NH: Heinemann.

Yancey, Kathleen Blake. 1992. *Portfolios in the Writing Classroom: An Introduction.* Urbana, IL: National Council of Teachers of English.

The Definition Approach: Turning a Have To into a Want To

All teachers have a book, a short story, or a type of writing that they *have to* teach; they are required to teach it. The mere mention of its title elicits deep, sympathetic groans: "You have to teach that? How dreadfully boring. I'm so sorry." No matter what teachers view as a *have to*, there is a way to make it more engaging for the students and more palatable for themselves. What follows is a model for using definitions that transform a *have to* into *want to*.

Michael discovered the Definition Approach when he had heard those groans one too many times. He needed a catalyst for teaching a unit that students would hook into and enjoy, so he decided to use the definition of *epic poetry* to teach Homer's *Odyssey*. Teachers can take this same approach with any *have to* in any curriculum.

In looking back at the steps Michael took to eventually come up with his unit, it is clear they grew out of a need to understand how to approach this large piece of literature so that students could connect to and interact with something that had been written more than thirty-two hundred years ago. Homer's *Odyssey* is a series of vignettes that follows Odysseus on his journey home to Ithaca and shows what he must do to defend his family once he arrives home. It is considered a *journey epic*. Michael understood *journey*, but he needed help with *epic*, so he turned to the definition in the textbook that he was required to use in his classroom. The generally accepted definition of an epic is a long narrative poem that tells the adventures of a hero or heroine who embodies the values of his or her civilization. With the definition as a wellspring, Michael eventually constructed how he would teach the literature, but more importantly, he now knew how to reach the students.

Michael's Experience

I like to reach students right where they live, root around in their cellars and unearth the beginnings of some great people. If through literature I can get them to share just a little bit of who they really are, or even discover who they are, since they often do not know yet, I think an assignment has worked. Both of the following writing assignments accomplish these goals.

Seeing that Homer's *Odyssey* was written more than three thousand years ago, I need an engaging way to catch their attention. I need to hook the students early, so I usually begin the unit by asking, "What's your definition of a good movie?"

"Blood!" one boy shouts out.

"Violence!" another chimes in.

"Good fight scenes are cool," one more sophisticated boy adds.

"A good romantic comedy," suggests a girl fed up with all of the free-wheeling testosterone in the conversation.

This goes on for a while, and I invariably sum up the conversation by saying, "So we need some solid action, neat characters that are interesting or fun to watch, and a dash of romance and excitement. As it turns out, that is almost the entire definition of an epic." After I share the definition, I summarize, "Homer's *Odyssey* has adventure, heroes, fight scenes, blood and guts, and a romance story all rolled up into one. That is the reason that it has stood the test of time for thirty-two hundred years."

I have made a connection from what they already know to what they need to know; now I need to clarify the definition a bit more with another definition. "Now, realize they didn't have television or movies three thousand years ago, so they had to have this *rhapsode*, a singer of tales that was the historian and storyteller of the time, go from village to village in Greece to tell about the adventures of a Greek hero named Odysseus. The rhapsode would sing the tales because that was more entertaining than just saying them, and all the while, the Greeks learned about the values that were important to their civilization."

At this point, as a rule, one inquisitive and bright student asks, "So an entertainer would go from village to village teaching everyone what was considered important to that civilization, and they did it all by putting values in a bloody adventure and romance?"

"Yep, and you did a great job using the definitions of both *epic* and *rhapsode* to define the situation. You listened well."

The hook is set, now I need to reel them in.

As the students read each adventure, they take notes on the actions, characters, and values shown by Odysseus. He embodies the values of his civilization, so we pay special attention to what he says and does throughout the epic. The students soon find out that many of the values that the Greeks held dear are still in place today: follow orders from your superiors or pay the consequences; curiosity can be both a good and a bad quality; honor your family; and home is where the heart is.

As a final assignment, I thought that the best way to be able to have the students show their complete understanding of the definitions of an *epic* and a *rhapsode* would be to create their own epic. But before I have them do this creative writing assignment, I have them sink their minds into reflecting upon the core of the definition of *epic* through a Values Take-Home Test. This test has one question: What values do you and your family have in common with Odysseus, as shown in Homer's *Odyssey*?

This assignment requires that the students take what we have read, discussed, and learned about values throughout this piece of literature and connect it to their own lives. I make sure to add in the phrase *and your family* because by having the students look beyond just themselves, I force them to dig deeper into the rich earth of their own values as well as those being taught and/or espoused by their family.

Over a few class periods, the students all share what they have written during a very in-depth class discussion that is very much like the Six-Million-Dollar Test dicsussed in Chapter 2. The best of the students comes out in these discussions because they freely share their faith, beliefs, values, and connections. The depth of these conversations has been enlightening and reveals the moral fabric that the students possess. Have there been students that shared little of themselves and their family, content to slide on the surface of the assignment and leave much of what they truly know and understand to the imagination? Sure, but these are the minority.

Now that the students have written about their own values, it is time for them to write about them through allegory. The actions that a student's hero will embody will be the values that the student wants to have the *villagers* learn. This is my basis for the Epic Writing assignment. The Epic Writing brings the entire piece of literature of Homer's *Odyssey* and the students' values together in one assignment. Now that the students have studied the Greek civilization and its values, it is time for them to bring it home and teach what they believe is important today.

I try to make this a grand event, so instead of a normal day where I hand out the assignment and go over the requirements, I announce the assignment with flair. "Welcome one and all! You have all been called to this place," I begin the class, "because you have passed the treacherous test of learning. You are now the newest rhapsodes of our civilization." In my best William Shatner acting style, I continue, "You are gathered here to use this time to finally write down our civilization's best stories that will teach all of the villagers of our land the values that we hold so dear. Now go. You have one week to write down your story. If you get writer's block, please use these guidelines to help you, for the best of your stories will follow each rule."

By this time, the students are not only hooked but reeled in and flopping on the deck of the boat, giddy to be caught.

I provide an Epic Writing check-off sheet that allows the students to make sure that they follow the definitions of both *epic* and *rhapsode*, check their progress throughout the writing process, and prepare themselves for the presentation of this assignment to the class. In the end, the definitions of *epic* and *rhapsode* rule the Epic Writing assignment and the presentation.

- In our textbook, an *epic* is defined as a long narrative poem that tells the adventures of a hero or heroine who in some way embodies the values of his or her civilization.
- The definition of a *rhapsode* is a singer of tales who is the historian and entertainer of his or her time. The entertainer portion of this definition is the most important of them all.
- Brainstorm what values you would like to demonstrate through a narrative story and performance. Make sure to write your entire story with the value of your hero or heroine (you) in mind. What is the value that is *embodied through his or her actions*?
- There is a limit to the time you'll have to share your wit, style, and dulcet tones. Briefly describe (in less than twelve words) the *one* adventure you will type on a maximum of two pages.
- List the gods who helped and hindered you during your adventure (have at least one of each).
- A *Homeric simile* compares a heroic event to an everyday event. For example: She swatted the speeding arrow away as easily as shooing a fly from a sleeping baby's face. In the lines below, write the one Homeric simile you have in your story.
- Your story needs to be grounded in today's civilization. Make sure to use the world around you and end your journey right here on campus. Did you conclude your epic in Mr. V.'s classroom/land? (required)
- Did you attempt the extra credit of putting your epic in poetic form? What was that form? Please attach a copy of the requirements or rules for that form. Any poetic form must be granted special permission from the head rhapsode, Mr. V.
- What is the due date of this assignment?
- What props will you use during the presentation and/or singing of your value story to the villagers that occupy this land (classroom)?
- Wear a toga and sign up for a food or beverage item as soon as possible for the party of all parties: the Celebration of Values!

Carol was the type of student who got ideas and concepts quickly, so to keep her interest for every assignment, she would always ask if there was something more that she could do. Since the extra credit was already built-in, after I handed out the Epic Writing check-off sheet, she left the room with a wry smile and a look of possibilities spinning in her head.

As I had expected, she came to class the next day with a plan, but she didn't want to share it in front of the class. She had been *ripped off* in the past by asking questions about her ideas out loud during class, so this time she wanted to bounce her concept off me alone. "Can I write the entire epic in haiku?"

"Remember, you have to have two typed pages."

"No problem," she replied confidently.

"Then go for it!"

The best thing was that this assignment was a challenge for her. Everything always came easily to Carol, but the requirements of the adventure, the heroine, the Homeric simile, the god that helped, and the god that hindered all played havoc with a syllable- and line-driven poetic style. She set herself up for the hardest assignment she had ever required of herself, and she loved every minute of it. I am so proud of her accomplishment! (See Figure 4–2).

Both the Values Take-Home Test and the Epic Writing assignment, accompanied by the Celebration of Values, are writing assignments that are deeply rooted in the definition of that type of literature. I have found that when I am required to teach something new but am unsure of how to teach the concepts, I look to the definitions for inspiration. I then try to look for that hook, that one experience that students can take away from class with a smile because they had some fun while learning or with a frown because it was so fun that it was over too soon. The Definition Approach reminds me that inspiration can come from the definition of the activity or concept itself.

How to Make It Happen

The activities mentioned in the previous section place the emphasis for learning upon the students by harkening back to the basics of the definitions. If the definitions are the key to the students' learning, the students must constantly go back to them as guidelines. In the Values Take-Home Test, students have to list those values shown or not shown by Odysseus and his men on their long voyage home. Students also have to connect their own values and those of their family to those demonstrated within the literature. Then, for the Epic Writing assignment, students have to write an epic of their own in which they are the hero or heroine who embodies a value of today's civilization. Lastly, they have to become a rhapsode and perform their value-filled epic to the villagers of their classroom in accordance with the definition of a rhapsode.

Journey

Once upon a time
An age ago in Japan
My story began:
It began slowly;
The itch to go exploring,
See my family.
In English Kingdom
They were, waiting for me to
Finish my schooling.
But no longer was
I content, so far from home
I prayed for advice.
The Decefemi.
Ten goddesses of all things,
Heard my heartfelt prayer.
Light and Dark aloof
Remained, as each chose their side:
Support, or Oppose?
Ocean came to me,
And told me to return home
If home I longed for.
Wood and Earth gave me
Supplies I needed, food and
Strong planks for building
And so I set out,
Sailing in a boat I had
Built with my two hands.
Wind granted passage
As smooth as if my ship
Sailed upon fine glass
While Ocean cradled
Me as a mother cradles
Her sleeping infant.
All was well, until
A great, three-headed dragon,
Ominous and black,
Reared its ugly heads
As it rose from the waves and
Ferociously roared

FIGURE 4–2. *"Journey" (Carol's Epic Writing)*

It snapped off my mast
Like a child snapping a twig.
I grew quite afraid.
But my supporting
Goddesses granted me a
Sword to slay the beast
A great strength arose
Within me, urging me to
Smite this horrid foe.
Though Fire, Storm, Ice, and
Steel conjured this obstacle,
I would defeat it.
I had not come all
This way, just to be stopped now,
So close to my home.
And thus I bravely
Leapt at my enemy, with
Triumph in my heart.
Set on victory,
I plunged my sword deep in the
Bosom of the beast.
As black blood spewed from
The dragon's chest, it shrieked in
Agonized defeat.
Exhausted now that
My task was done, I was borne
By a wave to shore.
When I awoke, I
Saw that I was in my bed,
Safe in my own home
Confused, I sat up.
My mother was there with me
She said I was home.
I cried for sheer joy,
Seeing that my journey was
Finally complete,
At long last I had
Reached the English Kingdom, where
I had longed to be.
Home with my parents,
My journey was complete, and
All was well and good.

FIGURE 4–2. *continued*

Throughout it all, the students have to make choices in their class work and their assignments while always coming back to the definitions because they rule the instruction.

1. When teachers are given a concept or piece of literature that they must teach, they can look to the definition for help and inspiration. The definitions of *epic* and *rhapsode* were the two that drove the assignments discussed here.

2. Teachers must pick out those areas of the definition that they believe will be most important to their students' learning. The word *values* seemed to jump out at Michael when he was first learning about Homer's *Odyssey*. He thought it would be a good inroad to the students' thoughts, beliefs, and home, especially since the point of the story was that Odysseus was trying to get home.

3. Teachers must pick out those areas of the definition that they believe will be least important to their students' learning. The word *long* in the definition of epic was not something that Michael wanted to require or encourage. There are only so many days in the year to read and grade writing, so placing a page limit on the assignment seemed the most logical for Michael and his sanity. Also, *long* is not necessarily a word that often promotes student engagement in learning.

4. If the writing can be something more than just another presentation, the teacher should look back to the time of the original concept or piece of literature to see if there are any easily executed tie-ins. Michael knew little of Greek heritage or culture, but he knew that every household has an old bedsheet that can be used for a toga. The Celebration of Values party described earlier is meant only to bring safety, levity, novelty, food, and drink to a potentially nerve-racking public speaking experience.

The Definition Approach to writing strongly involves students in choosing how they will go about presenting what they have learned. In the case of the epic poem, students don't get to choose what they read, but they exert control over how they will go about showing what they know in a way that encourages them to bring what is important to them and their family and/or community to the project. Students are able to produce a piece of writing that makes them focus on the goal of the assignment (the definition) but also flexes in providing opportunities for students to individualize their presentation of learning.

Adaptations

- This entire idea of planning around the definition is rooted in going back to the basics of the style of literature, writing, or concept. Any definition can be utilized to fit a teacher's need. Planning with the definition in mind can be very versatile. Michael was required to use the textbook on hand, and the definitions of both *epic* and *rhapsode* enabled him to create the assignments described previously. The possibilities for this type of planning are limited only by the openness to interpretation that the definition allows as well as the imagination of the teacher and students involved.
- Differentiated Instruction: Teachers may want to use a less complicated definition for ESE, ELL, or younger students to get them started. Depending upon the age of the students and the goal of the instruction, teachers can give a simplified definition and fewer requirements for the assignment. For example, an epic can be "a long narrative story that tells of an adventure of a hero."
- Students could create a pop culture response to Homer's *Odyssey* by creating a rap song or hip-hop dance that will tell the tale of their hero. Teachers can allow them to create their own modern-day epic or use the original plot as a guideline in creating a presentation that is more current with modern-day times.

Q & A

How does Michael read Homer's Odyssey *with his class?*

Michael reads the first adventure out loud to the class by himself. Then through the rest of Part 1, the beginning of Odysseus' journey home to when he arrives home, the group reads the text during class in a variety of ways, all of them out loud. For Part 2, the adventures on Ithaca, students begin by reading out loud in small groups and then they read silently for the last adventure. The idea is that the students are first introduced to the poetic style and then slowly gain independence with it. This method of progressively turning over the reins of control to students is especially helpful to ESE and ELL students when they have a teacher to guide them.

How does Michael explain the obvious marital indiscretions of Odysseus, who supposedly loves and honors his family so much?

This is a good chance to talk of the similarities and differences between the Greek civilization of 1200 BC and the students' world. What we might think is inappropriate today may have been perfectly fine, if not encouraged, back then.

Does the conversation of religion ever come up within the discussions or reading when it mentions gods?

Yes, and it is a great opportunity to talk about acceptance and appreciation of other cultures. It also allows students to think of a time before modern science, conveniences, and information and to logically try to understand why a people would subscribe to a religion that believed that there was a horse-drawn chariot that pulled the Sun across the sky.

Because the word poem *is in the definition of epic, if students decide not to be as elaborate as Carol, does this affect their grade?*

Not at all. Carol was a special case. Michael learned the hard way about this part of the assignment. When he first gave the Epic Writing assignment, he offered extra credit for those who wanted to write it in any poetic style without the requirement of checking in with him beforehand. Therefore, students just arbitrarily hit Enter when typing their papers to create what looked like stanzas and said that it was poetic blank verse. Though this was creative, it was just a way to take advantage of a loophole that has since been closed. Now Michael requires the extra step of asking permission for a particular poetic style, and he also does not allow blank verse as a poetic option. This part of the assignment is purely for those who want to go that extra mile.

Is singing a requirement?

No. It too is an extra-credit opportunity. Musical/Rhythmic is a multiple intelligence to which some students naturally gravitate (Gardner 1993), and Michael likes to at least offer this as an opportunity for those students that might be so inclined, even though no one has taken him up on it yet.

What if the students choose not to complete the assignment at home?

Students could brainstorm ideas in class of how they might answer the question at hand as well as possible examples from personal experience and familial contexts. Teachers could make time in class to have students write their answer based on this work already completed in class if for any reason the final assignment due date has passed.

What if a parent questions why a teacher is asking students to share family values?

It is within any parent's right to question the requirements of any assignment. If parents do not want to share this personal information with others, the teacher could ask the student to look to the community itself and answer the question by focusing on the values that her neighborhood or country espouses.

Scriptwriting

Scriptwriting is a unique brand of writing. It is the only writing that is meant to be seen and not read by its intended audience. —Unknown

One of the joys and pains of being a middle-level or secondary English teacher is reading student writing. Some of it is so good that one short piece can make a teacher's whole day. On the other hand, sometimes it is so atrocious that it makes a teacher question whether he is doing the students any good at all.

Many teachers have come to the conclusion that students' writing is often poor because they have not been thoroughly taught some basic, but important, methods for quickly improving their ability to tell a story. Some of the tools that students' writing could quickly benefit from are becoming hyperaware of the setting(s), knowing and developing the characters that inhabit scripts, and becoming proficient at using dialogue. Techniques for incorporating these into student writing can be difficult to develop.

An opportunity arose through the Florida West Coast Drama Festival for Terry's students to participate in a scriptwriting competition in which the winning script would be performed at the close of the affair. The festival required that scripts be in a format similar to one currently being used by screen and television writers called French's Format (examples will follow later in this activity).

Eventually, Terry realized that after students had tried Scriptwriting, many students' creative writing improved dramatically. As he examined portfolios, he noticed that the elements mentioned earlier had all improved naturally as a result of writing scripts. In subsequent years, Terry began to focus on these areas when teaching Scriptwriting and noticed even bigger improvements. Since then, Scriptwriting has become a staple of each school year's writing requirements.

Scriptwriting is engaging for students because they are highly interested in movies. Terry believes that if teenagers boycotted movies for one month, the movie industry would be on the verge of collapse. Students are the driving force of the movie industry, and this writing opportunity provides them a glimpse behind the scenes into the industry they so profoundly sustain.

Terry's Experience

Tony was reluctant about writing from the day he strolled into eighth-grade language arts. I could barely convince him to put his heading on his paper, let alone express himself in writing. When I felt it was time to expose students to the art of scriptwriting, I thought I was in for another battle just to get him by.

Boy was I wrong!

When I introduced Scriptwriting, I led students through some initial activities, but I spent time talking about a scriptwriter I know personally and his wild successes in Hollywood. This often gets students' attention. It really made Tony sit up in his seat! From this point on, when I asked students to try some of the preliminary writing activities that would lead to the ideas for writing scripts, Tony was one of the first students with their paper out and ready to go. I was intrigued, but I still thought this could be a passing phase.

The day we watched scenes from movies while reading the accompanying script pages, Tony approached me after class with an idea for his script. He imagined a story that began with a king being challenged for his crown and then a fight would ensue. He also shared some of the underlying story that made the idea interesting. He had never had any enthusiasm for writing to this point, so I wanted to harness this opportunity. I asked him to write a proposal for a script, no more than a page long. I tried to maintain his excitement by helping him see his idea make it to paper.

In homeroom the next day, Tony approached me with a *three*-page paper containing his story. The odd thing is that I still don't know if he realized he was writing. He had been so resistant previously that I was shocked that he would write on his own time.

Over the next two weeks, Tony worked industriously on his piece. His class had the option of working with a writing partner, but he chose to work alone. He asked his friends in and out of class and on the bus as well as his family to help him revise and edit. His mom emailed me to find out what was going on. Tony wasn't playing video games or watching television at home. In the end, Tony turned in one of the best scripts from any of my classes. His was chosen as one of the most adaptable to film, and one of four production crews was formed in his class to work with Tony, the director, to make his film.

During preproduction meetings the students assigned parts, planned costumes and props to bring from home, and ran through the scenes for filming. The day filming began, Tony's crew was the most prepared of any crew in any class. They quickly ran through each scene, carefully filmed and refilmed scenes, and after three class periods had produced a high-quality movie version of Tony's original work.

A few weeks later, at the awards assembly dubbed the Perrones, named for my school's principal, Tony's film took the award for best script. The kid who hated writing had won an award for his script. His smile stretched across his face until it looked like it hurt.

Mine too.

How to Make It Happen

Scriptwriting can become as complicated as a teacher wants to make it. The prewriting steps are very time-consuming, but they will save time in the end because the teacher won't have to explain and reexplain how the scripts are to be written.

1. Teachers should prime the pump before getting started. Have a discussion about favorite movies, the money that students pump into the movie industry, and how a story makes it to the screen. Students are naturally interested in this form of entertainment. They are the ones who keep the industry afloat. Terry always paints a picture for students so they see Scriptwriting as getting a behind-the-scenes look at the world they love so much. Teachers might include a discussion of general guidelines that students will follow, due dates, grading, and so on.

2. The second step of this process is to get students thinking about writing dialogue for characters. This is one of the strengths of Scriptwriting. It will focus students on writing good, clear, realistic dialogue for their characters. Terry focuses students on this because he expects students to carry this skill into other genres of writing later in the year. One of the activities that teachers can have students try is to write dialogue for two characters in a television show they like to watch. They can make things happen that might never happen otherwise. Another way to accomplish this practice is to find a show that is popular among your students and ask them to create one scene of dialogue. Make sure that the dialogue you provide will make students want to finish the story.

3. Next, teachers can find copies of scripts for some currently popular movies. These can be purchased in hard copy form online or downloaded for free from the Internet in many cases. The idea is to get a few scenes from some currently popular films that are also available on video. Teachers can show scenes from a video while students read the

appropriate pages from the script. This is a critical step because more often than not, it provides an "Ah-ha!" moment for students. They *see* the writing it takes to make the action on the screen happen.

4. Teachers should provide students with a handout that they can keep from a page of script used in class. This handout should have an example of the major types of formatting you expect students to follow when they write their script. Terry suggests a handout that contains formatting information for slug lines (scene headings), character description, action, and dialogue. These are the major features they will use in their scripts, but it is important to know that scriptwriting can become very complicated.

5. Prewriting can be as detailed as a teacher likes. At this point, students are often excited to get started. Terry suggests taking advantage of this excitement by asking students to define their characters well. To force students to deeply examine their characters, Terry uses an activity for story writing called the Character Interview, originally created by Elizabeth Babin, a colleague from the Tampa Bay Area Writing Project. During the Character Interview, students must conduct a brief interview with each of their characters using questions prepared by the teacher or by the class. This interview may contain questions that have nothing to do with the script, but the idea is to get students to think about and know their characters better *before* they begin writing. Students can create a list of appropriate questions, or the teacher can provide one. For five- to seven-minute scripts, Terry suggests limiting students to a maximum of three characters. More than this becomes difficult to manage for most writers in a piece this short. Many students, especially ESE and ELL students, might benefit from role-playing these interviews.

6. Teachers can ask their students to become familiar with the setting of their script before writing by asking them to draw or map out each setting. To make sure that students are aware of the settings within which their characters will interact, teachers may want them to do an aerial sketch or map of each setting they plan to include. This should be extremely detailed so that students know how the furniture might be set up in a room or where the tree that a character might hide behind is located in the park. More than two settings become difficult to manage in a five- to seven-minute script.

7. Next teachers may want to have students create a Power of Three for their story. This is a technique that has conflict begin a cycle, a

consequence for that action continue the cycle, and then a resolution to the conflict complete the cycle. Screenwriters often use the Power of Three as a technique to make sure that there is always something happening for a reason. Teaching this concept to students allows them to see that the action in their script always has purpose. Students must be able to defend why anything happens, and this cause-and-effect relationship forces students to state what happens clearly. Examples of the Power of Three are as follows: A man robs a bank; the police arrive; he is arrested. A patient comes into the emergency room; the doctors and nurses work to help him; the patient is released, dies, or goes to another part of the hospital. When students know what the major events of their story will be, they will then be able to fill the setting, characterization, and tone into their script. The Power of Three allows students to concretize those big pieces of their script so that the nuances of their writing can come through.

8. The final step of the prewriting process is writing the logline. A logline is simply a sentence that is not longer than thirty words that tells exactly what will happen in the script. Examples for this can be found in television guides where a description of an episode of a sitcom is provided. Students often view this like a piece of fiction. They must be reminded often that it is acceptable to give away the surprise ending in the logline. The logline is usually written to sell a script to a production company. In the case of student writing, teachers can use the logline to ensure that students have a clear idea of what will happen in their scripts. When writing a logline, students should consider who the main character is, what the problem he or she encounters is, and what the resolution of the problem is. This is a great check-off point. This is a chance for teachers to make sure that students have not overcommitted themselves for the length of their script. Students tend to get excited and will try to tell too much of a story for the length of the script.

9. Finally, it is time for students to begin writing (see Figure 4–3). Terry recommends having a final check-off point after students have written the first page. It is easy for a teacher to find and point out any formatting errors in a two-minute conference with a student. When this is done after the first page, it prevents the incorrect formatting from becoming a habit. The rest of the script should be correct. Students should be expected to follow the basics of script formatting. There are five basic guidelines students should follow, which can be readily seen in any Hollywood movie script:

A. Scene headings, or slug lines, should fall against the left margin and indicate that a new scene is beginning. They are always written in all uppercase and indicate the place and the time of day of the scene. For example:

```
INT. KRISTEN'S BEDROOM — EARLY AFTERNOON
```

B. Setting, character description, and action also fall against the left margin, and all character names and words that need emphasis are in uppercase. For example:

```
ZOOM TO CLOSE UP ON ABBY. ABBY is a good, safe,
and cautious fourteen year old girl. She has
blonde hair and blue eyes. She is very organized.
She is wearing jeans and a quarter length t-shirt.
She closes the magazine and sighs.
```

C. Dialogue is a challenge for many students to manage, but once they get the hang of the format, they find it easy and sensible. First, each letter of character names is capitalized and centered over their lines of dialogue. Also, the margins for dialogue are indented one inch from the left and the right of the rest of the script. When typing in Microsoft Word, this is done most easily by typing the dialogue, highlighting it, and then clicking and dragging the left and right indention markers found on the horizontal ruler at the top of the page.

```
                    ABBY
I'll go get my money, which is in my Louis
Vuitton purse.
```

D. The final guideline students follow is line spacing and typing requirements. There should be a line between all elements of scripts such as dialogue, action, and character description. Also, when students type a script, the industry standard uses Courier or Courier New font at point size 12.

10. Students should be given ample time to write. This is often their first experience with scriptwriting and they will need time to wrestle with the style and format of the genre. When the drafts of the scripts are done, it is time to edit and revise. Teachers may even add a step to this process during which students look at each other's writing only for formatting errors.

```
FADE IN:

INT. KRISTEN'S BEDROOM — EARLY AFTERNOON

LONG SHOT, EYE LEVEL PANNING BEDROOM. ROOM FILLED
WITH CLOTHES, SHOES, HATS AND JEWELRY. ROOM IS VERY
LIGHT AND THE WINDOW BEHIND THE BED IS OPEN, LET-
TING LIGHT SHINE THROUGH. TYPICAL GIRL'S BEDROOM.

ABBY is sitting on the bed, flipping through a maga-
zine looking very bored. KRISTEN is in a chair
going through her CDs', also looking bored. ASHLEY
is on the floor staring out the window trying to act
like she is having a good time.

ZOOM TO CLOSE UP ON ABBY. ABBY is a good, safe,
and cautious fourteen year old girl. She has blonde
hair and blue eyes. She is very organized. She is
wearing jeans and a quarter length t-shirt. She
closes the magazine and sighs.

                    ABBY
          So, what do you girls want to do?

PAN AROUND ROOM, ZOOM TO ASHLEY. ASHLEY is an out-
going rebel trying to be the center of attention.
She has brown hair and brown eyes. She is thirteen
years old. She is wearing a skirt and a spaghetti
string shirt. She continues to stare out the window
like she is in a trance.

CONTINUE TO PAN AROUND ROOM, ZOOM ON KRISTEN. KRIS-
TEN is nice, respectful, smart, and generous. A
typical thirteen year old trying to deal with life.
She is wearing capri jeans and an American Eagle
polo shirt. KRISTEN puts down her CDs.

ZOOM OUT FROM KRISTEN TO SHOW BOTH KRISTEN AND ASH-
LEY. ASHLEY and KRISTEN are looking at each other
and ASHLEY shrugs. ASHLEY smiles.

                    ASHLEY
          Hey! Why don't we go to the mall?

PAN TO SHOW ABBY AND KRISTEN. ABBY and KRISTEN
smile at each other.
```

FIGURE 4–3. *Abby's Script*

11. Once scripts are in final form, the teacher may publish them in a variety of ways. Students may get in groups and act them out, or the teacher or the class can choose several to be filmed. The important step here is providing an audience for this writing. Scripts are meant to be seen, not read.

Students will be highly engaged by the writing, and their focus on the dialogue, setting, and character development will be evident in the work they produce.

The amount of control and choice that you provide for students in this activity depends on a number of things. First, you must determine how much time you are going to dedicate to the process of Scriptwriting. Terry often spends about three school weeks in class on the project, with the expectation that students will spend time outside of class to do a spectacular job.

It also depends on your audience. If you teach upper-level, highly academic students, then you can certainly adjust the time you spend presenting this type of writing. If you teach students who struggle with writing, then you may want to stick to shorter pieces that will ensure their success.

All in all, Scriptwriting offers students a chance to try a type of writing that they may never get a chance to try again. Students enjoy the writing because they begin to see their ideas take shape as films in their mind's eye and this excites and engages them. Scriptwriting is something all writing teachers should consider adding to their repertoire.

Adaptations

- One obvious adaptation for including Scriptwriting is to begin with a unit on media literacy and film. It is important for language teachers to teach our students about all of the texts they will come into contact with in their daily lives and the techniques that are used to garner their attention. Some teachers may want their students to incorporate some of what they learned in the media literacy unit into their own scripts.
- Interdisciplinary Instruction: Teachers might work with a teacher in another discipline such as U.S. history and have students write scripts to re-create a part of history that students are studying.
- Another major adaptation that can be incorporated is to tell students that a number of scripts will be chosen to be produced. Terry now has teachers at his school read the best scripts and choose those that would best be adapted to film at school with minimal difficulty. Classes are divided into production crews, and filming begins. Once the films are complete, each class has a chance to view all of the films, voting takes

place based on particular criteria, and winners in several categories are awarded at a teamwide assembly. This has become an annual event that students and parents start asking about during the first weeks of school.

- Another adaptation is to allow students to work with a partner or two on the scripts. This benefits classes that include ESE or ELL students or resistant writers because they have more support built into the assignment. A *rule of three* could be used: it takes a good reader, a good writer, and a good communicator to come up with a good product, so allowing three students who each individually are strong in one of those areas helps all students in the group learn. Teachers can also create some kind of contract between students if teachers choose to allow this partnership. This also can benefit teachers in managing the paper load. If half of each class decides to work together, teachers might reduce the number of papers that need to be read by 25 percent or more.

Q & A

How is Scriptwriting scored?

A rubric is the fairest way to score this kind of writing. Terry usually has the rubric focus on dialogue, setting, characterization, formatting, directions, and final copy quality. Individual teachers must decide how these will be scored on an individual basis. Things to consider: Terry has found that it is most fair to err on the side of students when scoring scripts. Most students are turning in their first attempt at this kind of writing and should be given some latitude.

What if my students are reluctant writers?

Teachers can allow students to write scripts individually, in pairs, or in triads. A partnership can improve confidence for students and help teachers manage the paper load.

Further Resources

Because of the highly volatile nature of Web pages and their availability, we have not offered any specific Web pages here. We suggest searching on the Internet for sites that offer free copies of scripts and offer advice for writing better scripts. The amount and quality of this information is constantly changing.

Chapbook Project

The term *chapbook* derives from the chapman, the English name for a traveling bookseller from the 1500s to the 1700s. Among the literature chapmen sold were collections of notes—sketches of works by an author, poet, or artist on a single theme, subject, or idea that were put together in the form of a book. These books, referred to as chapbooks, serve as the inspiration for a fascinating combination of art and writing.

For students, the chapbook is a chance to look deeply into an idea, a theme, a concept, or a subject that captivates their imaginations and fascinates them as individuals. All students select an idea or subject and delve into it, immersing their imagination and creativity into it and exploring it in every way—with poetry, research, interviews, artwork, story writing, journal writing, photography, and any other relevant medium that occurs to them.

The Chapbook Project was inspired when Barbara E. Brown, a teacher at Middleton Middle School of Technology, visited a Tampa Museum of Art exhibit in which various Florida artists had created interactive books as art. She immediately thought that students could create these chapbooks in response to a theme that was important to them.

Barb's version of the chapbook asked students to include all of the art and writing listed earlier as well as some kind of surprise in the way they presented the chapbook.

This project, though trying at times, is one of the best overall projects Terry has ever conducted with students. It allows them so many avenues to communicate with an audience; it sparks creativity and compels students to set long-range goals. It also allows students to deeply explore a topic or theme that *they* find interesting. It is reminiscent of Ken Macrorie's (1988) I-Search paper but includes more varied methods of student response and creativity.

Terry's Experience

I told students about this project during the third week of school and explained they would have nearly the entire year to complete it in time for an installation in our school's makeshift gallery. The first major step was to generate a theme or topic that was broad enough to allow students a chance to explore many areas of a topic and to ensure there was enough to write about in order to avoid roadblocks throughout the writing process.

Throughout the year, I set aside days as chapbook workdays, during which students had to have particular aspects of the writing accomplished as well as show progress in the parent and community component of the project. Though the writing was obviously important to the completion of the assignment, this parent and community component was also important to its culmination.

The year of this project's inception involved a tremendous amount of learning for teachers and students. We were orchestrating a year long project whose foundation was not quite hardened yet. Teachers were adding specific details to the project in response to student work and suggestions. The first groups of students to attempt chapbooks were mature enough as students to give useful feedback to their teachers as to what would work and what might need to be adjusted.

They also were not shy about suggesting ideas to make our expectations less intrusive. Mary did her chapbook on veterinary medicine. This career was not a passing fad for Mary. She had applied to attend a magnet high school program in our district where she would receive hands-on training in veterinary science and graduate with a vet tech certificate. She also volunteered several hours a week in a vet's office near her home.

Mary was perplexed when we pushed her to interview someone who had the job she desired. Instead, she wanted to interview several people at the local Humane Society so that she could include the kinds of treatment that pets and animals tolerate from humans. Mary understood that this might not be directly linked to her chapbook topic, but she assured Barb and I that she would make it work. If she couldn't, she would interview a veterinarian and include this interview instead.

The interview became the most powerful part of her project. She had stories of animal abuse and the pets that were once loved and now stood in cages with no one to care for them. Her chapbook became a testimony of why she wanted to become a veterinarian, not an artistic examination of the career.

Frankie created a chapbook about the ocean. He spent a great deal of time each year in the Florida Keys boating, fishing, and diving with his family. He did extensive research on the environmental impact that humans are having on the Florida Keys and particularly the coral reefs that pepper the waters adjacent to the islands.

In the end, Frankie's chapbook was displayed in a crab trap. His *book* was interactive in that all of the writing he had done for his project was written on various types of fish and coral that he had created, colored, and cut out. He had even made them three-dimensional by making two of each, stuffing them and gluing them together. Each piece of writing was displayed on one of these puffy, colorful fish or coral from his favorite place: the ocean. When someone wanted to interact with his chapbook, she would reach into the trap, grab one of the fish, pull it out, and read it. They might have pulled out a poem, a photograph, a drawing, a story, a journal entry, or an interview, and each was artfully displayed on his artifacts in his trap. Though

Barb had a clear idea of the types of products students might create, Frankie's chapbook was the first example we saw that struck us as one that future students could look at to understand what we were asking them to do.

One of the experiences from a subsequent year that I would rather forget but that was extremely educational to me as a teacher was when Isaac wanted to focus his chapbook on the theme of safe sex. I was a little reluctant but thought, erroneously, that he should ask our principal to see if he thought this was appropriate. The principal gave Isaac permission to study this theme. I felt that this would give me deniability if anyone questioned the choice. I was right, but not completely.

Part of the assignment requires a surprise in how the chapbook is presented. Even I wanted to be surprised. I gave great examples to the students ahead of time, including Frankie's crab trap and stuffed fish, and I thought that I was covered. I was wrong. On the day the chapbook was due, students came running up to me, asking, "Have you seen Isaac? Did you see what his surprise is?"

Isaac had decided, with his mom's permission, that his chapbook should shock as well as educate its viewers. His writing was rolled up and stuffed or attached in various places on a blow-up sex doll. I learned the hard way to have students write a description of their surprise before bringing it to school. I tell them the surprise is for the gallery audience, not for me. My heart cannot take more surprises like that!

How to Make It Happen

1. The first step of the Chapbook Project is to introduce the concept of what students will be doing. This is an opportunity to discuss the aspects of the assignment, set the time frame, and help them start generating a theme or topic. Some students will want to do their project on whoever's music video is number one that week or their current favorite video game. It is important that they think about the long term. These kinds of topics go in and out of favor over a short period of time for adolescents, and the students will be begging in a few weeks to change their topic. During this decision-making process, one idea might be to generate lists of appropriate and inappropriate themes for chapbooks. Teachers might ask students to think about topics that have been with them for much of their lives. For example, if students have been taking dance for five years, some aspect of dance might be an appropriate topic. Choosing a topic should have a deadline just a few weeks from the day the project is presented.

2. Students should be given the minimum requirements for the project. For example, Terry requires the following for a yearlong Chapbook Project:

A. *Artwork (minimum of 10 items)*
   i. 1 original sketch, drawing, painting, and so on
   ii. 3 original photographs
   iii. 3 scanned pictures or photographs (these can be downloaded from the Internet)
   iv. 3 additional artistic pieces of your choice

These last 3 pieces of your choice can be three-dimensional, artifacts, or anything that you feel is relevant to your particular theme or subject.

B. *Writing (minimum of 15 items)*
   i. 3 original poems
   ii. 1 original piece of prose fiction (story, myth, legend, etc.)
   iii. 10 journal entries—the journal entries can include your comments on the process of putting your chapbook together, your reflections on what you discovered about your subject or theme, observations on what you're investigating, and so on
   iv. 1 interview—The interview will be part of the investigation process. You will find someone who is an expert on your subject or theme or who shares your interest in it.

C. *Research/Other Sources (minimum of 10 items)*

The chapbook must include references from other sources on your subject or theme.

   i. 3 poems by other writers
   iii. 2 prose pieces by another author, either fiction or nonfiction
   iv. 5 short quotations relating to your subject or theme from other sources (magazines, newspapers, books, letters, the Internet, etc.)

For each of these research sources, you must include the author's full name and the complete information about the source itself.

D. *Surprise!*

Each chapbook will include a creative and imaginative *surprise*. Consider this an opportunity to really exercise those creative muscles and include something we haven't thought of or to do something really unique with one of the categories listed above. *Surprise us!*

3. Once the topic has been generated, give students some time to work on artwork, writing, and research in class. They will need some specific direction in writing journals, conducting interviews, drawing, photography, and so on. (Terry often will have a photographer come

to class for a day to teach about taking professional photographs, which was originally suggested by a group of students.) Students need time to discuss their ideas with each other. The best ideas for creating chapbooks often happen when students are given the chance to discuss them with an adult and their peers.

4. Students must be given some direction in long-range goal setting. They need to use a planner or calendar to map out when specific assignments are due. They may need some guidance in how to plan this, as most of them will have no experience in realistically setting these types of long-term goals. ESE and ELL teachers are great resources to assist their students with these tasks.

5. Teachers need to have students generate ideas about the kinds of help they will need. The student suggestion mentioned earlier about having someone give a basic photography lesson impacted the class so deeply that Terry used it again in subsequent years.

6. A number of days are set aside to discuss students' progress, teach specific lessons they have requested, and give students time to work toward and meet certain checkpoints. The final nine weeks of the project are used to make final decisions about how the chapbooks will be presented. Some original ideas that students might have had earlier in the year may now seem either too grandiose or too bland for the scope and work involved in making their chapbooks come to life.

7. Dates are set for the gallery opening and invitations are sent out to parents and school dignitaries.

The Chapbook Project is the ultimate in providing students with control over their learning. They choose their topic. They choose what aspects of the project to work on and when. They choose how to present their work to an audience that goes beyond their classroom and school. These are all elements that help guarantee that students will be engaged with the project over the long haul. (See Figure 4–4.)

Adaptations

- Of course, depending on the time allotted for this project, a teacher may ask students to include all or just a few of the types of writing listed in the yearlong version of the chapbook. Terry suggests that teachers might want to reduce this project to a nine-week period the first time they attempt it. The yearlong version can be very overwhelming and is difficult to manage the first time around.

FIGURE 4–4. *Sarah's chapbook focused on fashion.*

- Teachers can encourage students to come up with additional categories of art or writing to include. They might even tell students that if they create a new optional category, they may exchange it for one equal item in the requirements. One of the goals of this project is to offer flexibility to the chapbook authors in the way they present their theme or idea. This kind of deal will encourage originality in chapbook presentation and might give teachers more ideas for options in the future.
- If teachers are set up to teach collaboratively with an ESE teacher, they may want to use the chapbook as a focused, short-term project or a *cornerstone activity*. A cornerstone activity is a long-term, independent assignment that each student must work on when he has finished the assigned task for any given day. As long as time is left within a class period, students are to work on this cornerstone activity. It would have a predetermined due date and could be tailored to each child's educational baselines.

Q & A

How do you make sure that students are progressing in their work on the chapbook?

Terry provides each student with a checksheet that lists all of the minimum requirements for the project. At agreed-upon points throughout the year, designated as chapbook workdays, students must bring new completed work to class. Terry has chosen to initial this checksheet when each item is completed. The nice thing about these checksheets is that one student might choose to do the interview first and another student might choose to write a couple of poems and then begin work on the prose. With this process, either of these is perfectly fine. The purpose of the checksheet is simply to ensure that students are making progress, as adolescents have a tendency to procrastinate.

How much of this assignment's writing is edited by the teacher?

Terry suggests that you gauge this according to your audience. It is very difficult to stay on top of helping students revise and edit everything throughout this whole process. Terry suggests that teachers allow students to do most of the revision and editing and offer to help only with real trouble spots. This way, students will get worthwhile practice in these processes while helping each other, and teachers will be able to manage the paper load.

Is each individual piece of writing, artwork, and research graded as a student finishes it, or is all of the work graded all at once at the end?

The teacher and/or the entire class can create a rubric for each part of the process or for the overall project. Terry has used rubrics for each individual piece of the project. Now, he has shifted to giving points for each checkpoint in the process and using a rubric for a major grade on the final product. This rubric includes plenty of opportunity for students to respond to the process of creating the chapbook as well as to have input into their own grade. Terry has rarely seen a chapbook that was of extremely poor quality. The learning is in the process, the long-range goal setting, and the deep investigation of a personally important theme. Grades are usually very good at the endpoint of this project, but more importantly, students have had an opportunity to grow over the course of a school year in various areas while working on a topic of their choosing.

Further Resource

Macrorie, Ken. 1988. *The I-Search Paper.* Portsmouth, NH: Heinemann.

5

Choice in Speaking

Anyone can stand up and speak in front of an audience; it is the fear of doing it that gets in the way. Interestingly enough, dependent upon where and when the survey is taken, the fear of public speaking is among people's top ten fears, right up there with fears of spiders, snakes, terrorists, the dentist, needles, heights, and death. Death? Some people are more afraid of public speaking than of their own mortality? Whoa!

Whether the audience is a small group of four students at a table or an auditorium full of family and peers, public speaking is an important skill to polish and develop in school. Teachers must provide students with the best possible conditions in which to learn this skill, as well as activities that will help alleviate their fears.

With this in mind, we offer several activities that might provide students with less stressful opportunities to speak in front of an audience. To ensure a safe atmosphere, teachers can offer students a very brief period to speak and a topic that is worthwhile about which they are the experts. The Identity Bag activity offers both by allowing students to talk about themselves. Another activity that is enjoyable for participants is Quick-Draw Public Speaking. When students haven't had much experience speaking publicly in class, this offers an opportunity to be silly while practicing a valuable skill. Many students see this activity as a chance to participate as well as a chance for the whole class to laugh. The element of choice in this activity is critical to its perceived safety. However, safety is definitely relative; what teachers feel is safe can be terrifying to their students. For longer speaking opportunities later in the year, after students have had a chance to hone their speaking skills, students need to be clear about expectations as well as have plenty of time to prepare and practice. The Poetry Coffeehouse includes all of these elements.

Identity Bag

Identity Bags provide a safe way for students who are normally uncomfortable speaking in front of a group to build confidence in their personal speaking skills. This activity is useful at the start of a school year as a way to get to know students quickly on more than an academic level. This activity sprang from Terry's shift from teaching about 60 students in the sixth grade to teaching at least 140 in the eighth grade. He was accustomed to having the chance to get to know his students during longer blocks of time and being able to hold regular individual reading and writing conferences. In eighth grade, however, it seemed to take forever to get to know students beyond their academic abilities, so he came up with the Identity Bag. An Identity Bag is simply a container that holds several personal items. These personal items should somehow indicate what is important to their owner; for example, a book might indicate a love of reading.

Terry has seen many versions of similar speaking activities, but this was a solution created in response to a problem. At the start of each year students spend the first part of several classes sharing their Identity Bags with their classmates and their teacher. It provides students the opportunity to speak for a short time in a new but safe environment about someone on whom they are the world's leading experts: themselves.

Terry's Experience

In the school year following the Columbine tragedy, Joe arrived at our school dressed in black from head to toe, including his eyeliner and nail polish. He had been kicked out of several other schools in our district, including an alternative placement school, and even though school had started several days before, he waited until now to finally show up.

We were worried.

The day he arrived was the last day my new students were presenting their Identity Bags. He sat in the back, asked reasonable questions, and seemed absolutely mesmerized by the idea of this mature version of show-and-tell. During the class I told him that if he liked, I would excuse him from the assignment since he was starting school later than other students, and I walked away. At the end of class, when everyone had left for his or her next class, he stayed back and asked, "Would you mind if I brought a bag on Monday?"

All of my teacher alarms were ringing. What might he bring? My mind swirled. "Ummm, you don't have to," I squeaked.

"But I want to. I want to let everyone know who I am. They look at me like I'm a freak, and I'm not."

"Sure. Bring it on," I replied hesitantly. I gave him the directions and a pass, and he left.

To say I thought about this over the weekend is an understatement. I wanted him to be successful at our school, but I was afraid he might use this public time to establish his reputation.

On Monday Joe walked in carrying a violin case and a small black bag and reminded me that he was going to present his Identity Bag. He went to the front of the classroom and began to share. First he pulled out a creased, worn photo of his mom and himself. He said that he loved her more than anything and that the patience she showed him through all the trouble he had been in could never be repaid.

After sharing a few more items, he placed the violin case on my overhead, opened it and pulled out . . . a violin. He told everyone that he had been playing violin (and *all* stringed instruments) for about two years. He proceeded to play a very intricate piece of music that was completely original. Hugely impressed, the other students gave Joe a standing ovation and then stopped when they realized he was crying. He was angry at himself because he had "messed up" a part of the piece, and he had wanted to play it perfectly. Everyone thought he had.

From that day on, I was one of Joe's biggest advocates. Over the course of the year, he became one of the best, most memorable eighth graders at the school. The kid who had been kicked out of several schools ended his eighth-grade year by applying to the most competitive high schools in our district. I like to think this turn for the better began with the Identity Bag.

How to Make It Happen

The Identity Bag is an incredible way to get to know students very quickly while giving them the chance to speak publicly on a safe topic in a safe place. Teachers often discover things about students that they would never have learned any other way. On the first day of school, teachers can create an Identity Bag of their own, following the directions they plan to provide their students, as an introduction to their classes. Following this introduction, teachers may hand out the directions and tell students when and how they will present their own bags. For these informal introductions, teachers may want to follow some variation of these guidelines:

1. Teachers should decide whether the container the students carry their items in should have importance. "I chose this grocery store bag because I like to eat!" or "I placed everything in this shoe box because of my love for shoes."

2. Next, teachers should decide on the required number of items. A good starting point is at least three items but no more than five. This allows students to speak for one to two minutes, not so short that they will reveal little about them but not so long that take up the first two weeks of school.

3. Students need specific examples and directions about the kinds of items they may and may not bring. Directions should include the following:
    A. Items should represent who you are and what is important to you.
    B. Items should have personal value, but not huge financial value. For example, bring a picture of the ten-thousand-dollar coin collection that your great-great-great-grandfather collected and passed down to you instead of the actual coins.
    C. Out of five items, you may bring only two photographs. Each photograph counts as an item. (Students sometimes will bring a heap of photos [a photo of their cat, a photo of their house, and a photo of their favorite pair of shoes] and try to count them all as *one* item.)

4. Students always seem more comfortable once they know the particulars of any assignment. They will need to know *how* they will present. Do they need to be in the front of the class? Can they stand at their desk? Will they be allowed to pass items around or just show them as they are removed from the bag? How will this assignment be graded?

5. Teachers should decide when students will present. Will everyone be required to speak on the same day? Will they be allowed to bring their bag on any day over a range of days? Will they have to sign up for a particular time slot?

In the version of this assignment just described, students might control the number of items they bring, and the specific items they bring, which controls what their audience finds out about them. In addition to the choices they have, they are also speaking on a topic about which they happen to be the number one expert out of the six billion people on the planet.

Powerful? Yes!

Engaging? Yes!

Adaptations

- This assignment can be adapted for sharing books. Students decide which three to five items would best represent their book and then present a Book Talk (see this activity explained later in this chapter) in the same way the Identity Bag is presented.
- Another variation would be to do a Book Talk as a character from a book. If there is a literature circle reading a book, each member of the group can be a character and present an Identity Bag as that character. This will give the rest of the class a great picture of what the book is about.
- Interdisciplinary Instruction: You can make this activity multidisciplinary by teaming up with a history teacher, for example, to have students present bags based on time periods or biographies. Students could earn credit in history for the content and in language arts for the speech itself.

Q & A

What can teachers do if on the first day of presentations, no one brings a bag?

The teacher should remind the students that one of the pleasures of the Identity Bag activity is being part of the audience, finding out information about each other that they didn't know before. It is also encouraging to tell them what a relief it is to be finished and to be able to be an audience member while the rest of one's classmates present. This is usually enough to get a nice turnout the next time the class meets.

How do I grade this assignment?

Teachers can grade the Identity Bags in whatever way best fits into their philosophy and style of teaching. A participation grade is usually enough to get students involved. They like talking about themselves, no matter how they feel about speaking in front of each other. Almost always, the desire to tell people about themselves overrides any fear of speaking in front of the class.

What about the students who are just too scared to do this assignment?

These students could come by during lunch to present their Identity Bag to their teacher. Depending on the goal for the assignment (getting to know the student), this might be acceptable. If the goal for them is to present information to the rest of the class, an alternative might be to help them find another method or to co-present with a friend from class.

Students need the experience of speaking publicly but not at so great a cost that they don't trust their teacher in the future.

Quick-Draw Public Speaking

The Quick-Draw Public Speaking activity allows students to practice speaking publicly for a very short period of time in a safe environment about a topic that allows them to be clever, funny, and creative.

Terry was having trouble with students relying on too many vocal or verbalized crutches like *um, err, ah, like,* and *you know* when they presented prepared information to the class. One of Terry's colleagues, Pete Fuentes, suggested that Terry adapt a speaking activity that he often used in his U.S. history class that invited students to address the class on a topic they did not know about until just before speaking. It is used as a game to see who can speak using the fewest number of these crutches. This is a valuable activity in any public speaking unit because it forces students to become hyperaware of these crutches, discuss which words and sounds are used as crutches, and then start to shave them from their verbal repertoire.

Terry's Experience

Ann Marie stood up to present her part of her group's literature circle project on Susan Draper's *Tears of a Tiger.*

"So, ummm, when they drank alcohol, errr, the, ummm, you know, after the game, then they went driving, and they, like, you know . . ."

And so it went. I cringed as the hairs on the back of my neck stood up and the audience degraded into a mob of thirteen-year-olds who were either drooling or counting the number of holes in the ceiling tiles.

Something had to be done.

The next time Ann Marie had to speak in front of the class, she did much better. She even commented on her use of crutches: "I think I only used two crutches, Mr. B.!" Her smile showed her pride at making huge strides in her ability to speak publicly. The Quick-Draw Public Speaking activity had made her aware of her speaking crutches, and she had learned to eliminate them from her public speaking persona.

How to Make It Happen

The Quick-Draw Public Speaking activity is simply done by classroom teachers. After a brief discussion of crutches and the way they impact a speaker's effectiveness, it is time to make it happen in the classroom.

1. To introduce this speaking activity for the first time, teachers pull a topic out of a hat or container and intentionally use tons of crutches to speak about it as a nonexample. This leads to a discussion about effective speaking and what these crutches can do to even the best-prepared speakers.

2. Teachers should then ask for a volunteer to pull another preprepared speaking topic out of the hat. Topics should be narrow enough so that the student only needs to share for thirty seconds or so. Possible speaking topics could include the following:

   - Tell about the time you were given a Ferrari for a day.
   - Tell about the time you were in charge of a taco factory.
   - Tell about a time that you were your best friend's book bag for a day.
   - Tell about the worst (appropriate) dream you ever had.
   - Tell what the *best day ever* would be like for you.
   - Tell about your favorite food and why it is your favorite.
   - Tell about a holiday you think we should celebrate, but that we don't . . . yet.
   - Tell about an item you hope is invented in your lifetime.
   - Tell about your favorite class and why it is your favorite.
   - Tell about the job you want to have when you leave school.

3. Teachers must choose a student to be the timekeeper; he or she will tell the speaker when to start and stop. The teacher or another student can take over this job if the timekeeper chooses to speak during the activity.

4. Teachers then choose two crutch counters. Each will need a sheet of paper and something to write with so he or she can tally crutches as each speaker takes a turn.

5. After the first student has spoken on the topic for a predetermined amount of time, that student should be told the number of crutches utilized and also should be congratulated on a job well done as well as commended for bravery for going first. Teachers can repeat this process with one or two more students before the next step.

6. Next, students will need one, two, or even five small slips of paper.

7. Teachers then direct students to write their own creative speaking prompts.

8. After collecting the prompts in a hat, teachers may challenge students to choose a topic and give each a few seconds to prepare to speak.

9. Once a student has chosen to speak, the timekeeper will be the only one to begin and end the student's speaking.

10. Each student speaks for the allotted time period; the crutch counters report on the number of crutches in the speech, and the next person can choose a topic.
11. Teachers should leave time at the end of the period for debriefing.

One of the best qualities of this assignment is the fact that students are not forced to participate. The simple challenge and fun of the activity drives the learning. Most students will want to participate even the very first time this activity occurs in class. Students love the challenge of trying to beat their peers as well as master the problem. They are able to laugh at themselves when they make a mistake, and most students want to try again to beat the game.

In subsequent classes, all students will have participated except the most reluctant ones, and these students are so fearful of being the focus of attention that forcing them to participate will not do them any good. It is important to find a way to get them to take part, however. One way to do this is to speak to them before class begins and invite them to participate during class. If necessary, the teacher may even offer these students a chance to draw a topic in advance so that they can prepare to speak. The goal is to get students to try. Once they have done this, they will likely want to try it again.

Adaptations

- If teachers are studying a particular unit (relationships, hate in the world, etc.) or a novel, they can create the speaking topics in advance and tell students that the topics are about the unit. Students will then speak and hear opinions and information about the topic from each other.
- If teachers are working on a speaking unit, teachers may require students to participate for a grade or for extra credit.
- Everyone might count crutches to help listeners maintain focus in classes that lose focus easily.
- Interdisciplinary Instruction: Teachers might collaborate with history, science, or even math teachers in developing topics. While students are practicing being aware of crutches, they can be reviewing information from other disciplines.
- Teachers can adjust the time that students have to speak. If they are inexperienced, thirty seconds to one minute is fair. As they become experienced, the teacher may increase the time.
- Students can *name* a time. "I can speak about this topic for ___ seconds." This can be an added element of fun and challenge to this activity.

Q & A

What do teachers do if no student is willing to participate initially?

Once teachers break the ice, students feel the challenge of beating their classmates. If teachers decide to run this activity for a participation grade or extra credit, maybe doubling the points available for the first person (or first three people) who volunteer is an option. Once they start, there will be no stopping them. They will beg to do it in the future.

What can teachers do if they find that some of the student-generated topics are inappropriate?

The authors have encountered this problem and the solution is simply to allow the speaker to draw a topic and hand it to his teacher first. The instructor can then read it and, if it's inappropriate, have the student choose again. This also allows the teacher to ensure that each speaker receives a speech-worthy topic.

What if the topics students created just aren't that good?

If teachers suspect that the students might not have a handle on creating good topics, teachers can prepare slips in advance to add to the mix (a good start can be found in the How to Make It Happen section). By adding these to the slips created by their students, teachers then know that some of the topics will be good. Another option is to use teacher-created speaking topics to start the speaking and, once these run out, ask students to create more. With practice, students will be able to suggest quality topics that will be worth speaking about for their classmates.

Book Talk

The Book Talk curbs the fear of speaking by creating a safe atmosphere while also holding students accountable for the content of their most recently read book. It also allows for the practice of the important speaking skills of projection, enunciation, stance, and presence while working on persuasive techniques.

Michael has seen many forms of this assignment from noted authors like Linda Rief and Nancie Atwell, and his version of this classic assignment is gleaned from them as well as others.

Michael's Experience

I often had to ask Leslie to speak up in class. If I asked students to line up by physically placing themselves in alpha order by their middle name or in alpha order using a descriptive adjective, when it was her turn to speak, Leslie would politely whisper her answer, barely loud enough for the person next to her to hear.

Each time I would gently remind her that she needed to speak clearly by projecting her voice to the back of the classroom. "Peel the paint off the wall behind me with the power of your voice," I would joke. "I'll tell you if you are too loud." She would smile because I had tried to take the edge off of the public speaking moment, but at the same time, I knew that she would much rather have had me move on to the next person in line instead of drawing even more attention to what she considered her biggest fault. Eventually she would chirp her answer, barely stronger than a sigh, and then look at the next person in line as if to say, "OK, time to go on to the next person." I knew that the Book Talk assignment was coming soon, and I needed a way to hook Leslie as well as the entire eighth-grade class.

Demonstration time. I must admit that I have a flair for the dramatic, so it was not a surprise to my students that after I handed out the directions and grading rubric for the Book Talk, I broke into character.

Holding a copy of Bradbury's *Martian Chronicles* at my side and lightly tapping it on my left leg, I stood in front of the class, stared at the carpet in front of me and projected the following with my best speaking voice: "OK, I read this book titled *The Martian Chronicles*." I shifted my weight to the right and paused for an uncomfortably long moment. "I read this book and you should read it because it is good." Again a long pause, but I shifted my weight to the left this time. I continued with my rich speaking voice, "I actually didn't really understand a lot of it, but I like to read 'bout aliens and stuff, so it's good." I started wringing my free hand within itself and twitching my face as if I had just developed a facial tick on my right cheek. After another five-second pause, I concluded, "So if aliens are something you like, though it was really nothing like any cool movie or TV show I have ever seen, then you should read the book." I ended by rigidly holding the book out, forcing a no-teeth smile, and staring at the table of four students directly ahead of me.

Snapping back to myself, I announced, "By looking at the rubric that I handed out for the Book Talk, please grade the presentation that you have just witnessed. Please be fair but tough." I got high scores for projection, but on everything else students felt I needed to do much better.

Invariably a student will ask, "So if that was a nonexample, can we see an example of one that covers all of the highest marks on the rubric?"

"No, you may not," I quickly answer. "We have practiced every one of these skills as well as discussed each facet in class for the last several weeks. You have the rubric. Go from there."

Discussion does continue about persuasiveness as well as how to capture a class' attention, but I try to be vague enough so that they make their own decisions about how they will present individually.

When the day finally came for the presentations, students had already written and practiced their Book Talks in class, so this was the final evidence that they indeed had not only read the book but had also practiced all of the speaking techniques we had studied in class up to that point in the year.

Leslie sat in her seat and lightly ran her upper teeth over her bottom lip. This was her only sign of nervousness because she sat a little straighter in her chair than normal and had crisp and neatly printed note cards in her hand. When it was her turn, a light came over her face, she grabbed the copy of her book, and she put the note cards down on her desk (note cards were an option, but memorization was encouraged). I was shocked that Leslie had taken the leap.

She loved the book that she had read, and her passion for reading it came out. She read an excerpt from the middle of the book, a particularly eerie and richly spooky description of a vampire trying to seduce his next victim. Her voice was still soft as butterfly wings, but because of the conviction of her delivery, she commanded the room. She ended at exactly ninety seconds, the longest the speech could be, and sat down with a huff and a sigh, all the while smiling. Leslie had taken the leap because she knew that this was an assignment that offered choice in presentation. When we debriefed the assignment after each student had performed, Leslie shared, "I hate public speaking, but everyone had to do it. I had the rubric ahead of time, and I wanted to make sure everyone heard about my book. I'm glad I did it." And the class was better off that she did.

How to Make It Happen

1. The teacher needs to decide which skills will be graded for the Book Talk. Michael focuses on voice projection, word clarity and enunciation, and stance and presence.
2. After the teacher has chosen which skills to grade, he needs to define a way of grading those areas. Michael uses a number line rubric that has word explanations for the low, middle, and high ability for each skill. Each skill has a gambit (a beginning of a sentence with an ellipsis) and then three sentence completions. For example, for projection,

the rubric states, "Your projection made you sound like you were . . ." score one, ". . . a mouse," score three, ". . . talking to someone nearby," or score five, ". . . involved and knowledgeable." It is possible to speak softly and still be involved and knowledgeable, so some information about a student can be taken into account.

3. The teacher should also include areas that deal with content. Is an introduction important? Will examples or excerpts be required or optional? What is enough information to show that the student has clearly read the book outside of class?

4. The teacher also needs to set a time limit. If students are given free will to ramble on and on or are forced to say too much in too little time, the assignment loses it power. When the teacher gives a specific time frame, it requires the student to practice and make sure to get to the point as well as include only that information that will have the greatest lasting effect.

5. The assignment must be handed out weeks before the speeches will occur. In Michael's experience, springing a speech on students is a recipe for disaster. Public speaking is what it is, so if time is built into the schedule for students to ask questions, write, practice, and ask more questions, they will feel that much more prepared. An example of Michael's directions are as follows:

> The Book Talk is a culminating activity that shows that you have read your book as well as been working on your presentation skills. You will be trying to entice your fellow classmates to want to read the book that you have finished reading for your Reading Contract. You will do this by presenting a Book Talk to the class. You will present a *talk* that is between eighty and ninety seconds in length. During this presentation, you will use your persuasiveness to encourage and interest the students in your class to want to read your book. Remember, you are not only persuading the students but also practicing everything that we have worked on this year with projection, enunciation, and stance. Use the rubric to see exactly what you will need to prepare as well as how you will be graded on this information. Most of all, remember to have fun!

6. On the day of the Book Talks, the teacher may opt to start the class with an icebreaker activity that will get each student up, moving, and speaking to others informally. This cuts the tension of the day and helps create a positive atmosphere in the room.

7. The teacher must address ground rules about what is appropriate class-room etiquette for an audience to continue the tone of the day. If the teacher can create a safe atmosphere of acceptance and approval, the talks should be able to go off with control and grace. If it is physically possible, students who are unable to verbally and/or nonverbally show their gratitude for every speaker need to be removed from the class so that those who can will enjoy the fun and gain the benefits of presenting to an appreciative, positive audience.

When students choose a book, they are often afforded a wide range of choices, and though students do not have the choice about which book they will present to the class for their Book Talk, they do have a choice in what they will say and how they will deliver it. Will a famous quotation really get their audience's attention, or will reading a passage from the book grab and hold their audience the way they want? The idea is to persuade their peers to want to read their book, and individual students must decide how best to sell it.

Adaptations

- The talk need not be about a book. This same structure can be used as a review for a test.
- Interdisciplinary Instruction: This structure can be used to present each of the major players for a social studies, Spanish, or math unit, either as a culminating activity or as an anticipatory set.
- Differentiated Instruction: Time is always a factor that can be changed for the assignment. Many small speaking assignments of fifteen to thirty seconds can lead up to a sixty- or ninety-second presentation.
- Differentiated Instruction: Teachers could grade the assignment on just one skill at a time. If projection is the skill that the class needs to work on the most, small versions of this assignment could work solely on that skill and then branch out to others as the students show improvement.
- Presenting on camera is an entirely different animal. A teacher might think that adding a camera to the back of the room would just capture the happenings of the class that day, but interestingly enough, it adds more pressure to the situation. It is a perceived threat because placing a presentation on tape creates a feeling of permanence instead of something fleeting. A teacher must think over the rationale of taping the assignment and allow the students to know ahead of time if their

speeches will be recorded. If the teacher also shares exactly how the tape will be used, the students will at least know ahead of time and can prepare for it.

- Students could have the option of taping themselves at home and bringing in the completed assignment. This takes away the *public* in the public speaking assignment, but the teacher must decide what skills are more important to evaluate and go from there. Teachers can also look into the availability of a video camera at school or set up a time during the day, before, or after school that students could come into class to complete this assignment. The teacher needs to decide what lengths will be taken for each student to find success with this skill.

Q & A

What if a student refuses to give a talk?

A teacher could let the student present the talk to the teacher one-on-one at another time or videotape the speech at home.

What if the student has yet to complete the book by the date of the talk?

The student should be held accountable for the completion of the assignment. If after a prescribed time the assignment is left undone and all other means of having the assignment completed have been exhausted, then the student has earned the zero. However, if zeros are not an option, maybe the student can do a Book Talk for the amount of the book that she has read so far, with the understanding that a makeup Book Talk will be required when she has finished the book or when she has completed a new book in which she has more interest.

What if the student is obviously lying abut the book's content and fakes a report?

This is a professional dilemma. Some teachers may fail the student for the assignment and leave it at that. Others would see this as an opportunity to work with the student and require him to complete the reading of the book and present a new Book Talk. Parents and administration may be able to help in this situation.

Why use persuasiveness instead of just exposition?

If students have to analyze a book to find a way that will make it appealing to an audience, they are activating a deeper schema than that of just *telling* about the book. Students need to know this, and teachers can explain it up front instead of tacitly.

What if the student doesn't like the book?

This is a situation that can be troublesome but has a simple solution. If a student has read an entire book but does not like it, requiring her to say who would like it and why is the best route. This requirement can stretch students to think of advertising and all of those items in the mall that some of their friends really love and others find repulsive. It is a good lesson in persuasiveness to require that they try to promote a book to an audience that would truly like it even though they personally did not.

Poetry Coffeehouse

Performance of literature brings the written word to life, and poetry is the one form of literature that carries with it the scope of human emotion in compact and quickly accessible bites. The Poetry Coffeehouse is a wonderful vehicle to showcase students' learning about words, ideas, genres, life, and performance. It is a celebration of poetry and life through performance. Students perform a poem of their choice on a night full of groovy beatniks, syncopated jazz, and strong coffee. Overall, the coffeehouse can be used as a culminating event to a poetry unit in any grade, and it allows students the ability to grow as students and as people.

Michael's Experience

During six years of creating Poetry Coffeehouses, the event has been classified by many parents and students as the one event they enjoy the most. I am proud of what it has become. The coffeehouse asks students to constantly read poetry for one month in different ways: during class with provided books, with the teacher with provided handouts, at the library with books pulled out by the librarian, and on their own at home, curled up on the sofa with their books and/or seated in front of their computers, reading on the Internet. It took a while for the students to really want to read poetry, but the more I required it and the more they did it, the more they got into it.

After this intensive reading, I give out the requirements for the Poetry Coffeehouse. The requirements usually fit on a half-sheet of paper and detail all of the deadlines and specifics of the assignment. I request that students choose three poems that they would feel comfortable performing in front of others, namely in an auditorium designed to look like a late-sixties coffeehouse on poetry night, filled with two hundred friends, students, and parents. The most important word is *performing* because this is not a poetry reading or recital. Students are to memorize their poem and take on the characters, setting, and movement that the poem contains.

The following are the requirements I distribute about choosing a poem for the Mid-March Poetry Coffeehouse event.

1. Choose three poems that you would enjoy performing (you will perform one).
2. They must be published poems found in books.
3. They must have a minimum of fifteen lines.
4. The English teacher(s) must approve each poem (the coffeehouse needs variety).
5. You may perform poetry at the coffeehouse with up to three other people.
6. If teaming, each part must have a minimum of fifteen lines.
7. Copies of your poems with all of the performers' names written clearly on the back are due _____. Have a copy of each poem to turn in as well as one for each member of your group.
8. Shel Silverstein and Jack Prelutsky are reserved for sixth-grade performers.
9. Have fun reading!

"Casey at the Bat" by Ernest L. Thayer, is shown in Figure 5–1. The setting is that of a baseball park on a grim afternoon. The characters of narrator, Flynn, Blake, Casey, ballpark fans, the pitcher, the catcher, and the umpire are all represented by specific descriptions and actions that Thayer has created. The action includes but is not limited to a pitcher throwing pitches, batters getting hits and running the bases, an umpire calling strikes, fans calling out how they feel, and, of course, Casey swinging his bat. The poem rules the day. Whatever the poem says, the students must interpret those words into characters, settings, and actions.

To teach my students about performing poetry and prepare them for the Poetry Coffeehouse, I invited Poetry Alive, a wonderful performance organization that each year brings poetry to life for thousands of schoolchildren throughout the United States, to our class. Poetry Alive treated us to an hourlong demonstration of poetry performance and then came to the classroom to explain how they did it. Overall, the Poetry Alive members explained that the characters, settings, and actions of the poem, as defined by the poem, are the building blocks of the performance, but they also explained to my students and me that animals, objects, and even sounds can come to life when performing a poem as well.

Casey at the Bat
by Ernest L. Thayer

The outlook wasn't brilliant for the Mudville nine that day,
The score stood four to two, with but one inning more to play.

And then when Cooney died at first, and Barrows did the same,
A pall-like silence fell upon the patrons of the game.

A straggling few got up to go in deep despair.
The rest clung to that hope which springs eternal in the human breast.
They thought, "If only Casey could but get a whack at that.
We'd put up even money now, with Casey at the bat."

But Flynn preceded Casey, as did also Jimmy Blake;
and the former was a hoodoo, while the latter was a cake.

So upon that stricken multitude, grim melancholy sat;
for there seemed but little chance of Casey getting to the bat.

But Flynn let drive a single, to the wonderment of all.
And Blake, the much despised, tore the cover off the ball.

And when the dust had lifted,
and men saw what had occurred,
there was Jimmy safe at second and Flynn a-hugging third.

Then from five thousand throats and more there rose a lusty yell;
it rumbled through the valley, it rattled in the dell;

it pounded through on the mountain and recoiled upon the flat;
for Casey, mighty Casey, was advancing to the bat.

There was ease in Casey's manner as he stepped into his place,
there was pride in Casey's bearing and a smile lit Casey's face.

And when, responding to the cheers, he lightly doffed his hat,
no stranger in the crowd could doubt t'was Casey at the bat.

Ten thousand eyes were on him as he rubbed his hands with dirt.
Five thousand tongues applauded when he wiped them on his shirt.

FIGURE 5–1. *"Casey at the Bat"*

Then, while the writhing pitcher ground the ball into his hip,
defiance flashed in Casey's eye, a sneer curled Casey's lip.

And now the leather-covered sphere came hurtling through the air,
and Casey stood a-watching it in haughty grandeur there.

Close by the sturdy batsman the ball unheeded sped—
"That ain't my style," said Casey.

"Strike one!" the umpire said.
From the benches, black with people, there went up a muffled roar,
like the beating of the storm waves on a stern and distant shore.

"Kill him! Kill the umpire!" shouted someone on the stand,
and it's likely they'd have killed him had not Casey raised his hand.

With a smile of Christian charity, great Casey's visage shone,
he stilled the rising tumult, he bade the game go on.

He signaled to the pitcher, and once more the dun sphere flew,
but Casey still ignored it, and the umpire said, "Strike two!"

"Fraud!" cried the maddened thousands, and echo answered "Fraud!"
But one scornful look from Casey and the audience was awed.

They saw his face grow stern and cold, they saw his muscles strain,
and they knew that Casey wouldn't let that ball go by again.

The sneer has fled from Casey's lip, the teeth are clenched in hate.
He pounds, with cruel violence, his bat upon the plate.

And now the pitcher holds the ball, and now he lets it go,
and now the air is shattered by the force of Casey's blow.

Oh, somewhere in this favored land the sun is shining bright.
The band is playing somewhere, and somewhere hearts are light.
And, somewhere men are laughing, and little children shout,

but there is no joy in Mudville—
mighty Casey has struck out.

FIGURE 5–1. *continued*

What Was That!?

I couldn't sleep. I held my breath.
It helped me to listen. I clutched my chest.
What was that? Oh my, could it be?
The sound that makes all children pee?

Moms and Dads, they must not care
Or can they hear what children dare?
They've grown too old to hear the sounds
Of quick Saint Nick coming to town!

FIGURE 5–2. *"What Was That!?" by Michael J. Vokoun*

In the poem "What Was That!?" (Figure 5–2), the sounds that are heard at night could be characters acted out by many different students. Are these spooky and dreadful sounds, and what do these sounds look like onstage? The nice thing about this poem is that readers, and eventually the students who perform this poem, have to use their imaginations to decide what noises would keep a child awake at night. It is not until the last line, when it is revealed that the sounds are associated with Saint Nick, that the poem takes on an entirely different feel. That fact can be exploited in the poem's performance. This exercise opened the door to a myriad of opportunities on how all poems can be performed and allowed students to delve deeper to find those surprise moments to put into their own presentations.

Also, students must look at their poem after they have decided who their characters are and then choose which of these characters is saying what line when the poem doesn't explicitly state who is saying what. For example, in "What Was That!?" the narrator "I" can be a character who narrates the entire poem, or each sentence could be spoken by a separate child who is having the same trouble sleeping. Are they all in the same bed, or do they each hear different types of sounds? Mom and Dad could even be onstage, sleeping and not caring, or they also could be the ones making the sounds by taking out the hidden presents and placing them under a tree. This exercise shows that interpretation is within the eye of the beholder, but it brings up an important point. The poem rules the day, and as long as the choices that the students make are within the spirit of the poem, the choices are right. Some students come up with great ideas for the performance of their poem, but a few of the lines would need to be altered or deleted to make their idea fit. I always explain to them, "The poem rules the day; only what is in the poem can become reality onstage."

Some poems can be interpreted appropriately or inappropriately based solely upon the student. The teacher is the determining factor in all of it. This is one reason I have the students submit three poems. The students must choose three poems as well as what actions would be appropriate for their audience. If they think of characters, setting, and action ahead of time, students will have more of an opportunity to be happy with whatever poem they are ultimately told they must perform.

Also, I have students submit three poems because many students of the same age have similar tastes in poetry. If many students submit the same poem and it meets the basic requirements of the coffeehouse, I can decide which of those students will get the opportunity to perform it. The other students and I now have at least two other options from which to choose.

When it comes to poetry, some students have chosen poorly in the past. Many conversations a few days before the coffeehouse have gone something like this. Usually looking at the ground or at something fascinating on his shoe, a student will say, "I haven't memorized my poem because I hate it. I don't get it. I know it's only a few days before the coffeehouse, but can I pick a new one?"

I calmly get out the information about his poem selections and say, "It says here that you got your first choice."

"Yeah, but I didn't read it before I turned it in."

I blink twice, giving some time for that information to sink in, and continue, "The directions say, 'Choose three poems that you would enjoy performing.'"

"Yeah, well I just found three fifteen-line poems in a book that I found on a shelf in my house."

"I am sorry to hear that."

"So can I switch?"

"Nope."

In every instance, I show students that they made the choice to turn in their poems. If they choose to forego the suggestions that have been modeled and discussed in class by me or by Poetry Alive then they have to live with those choices.

One choice that several boys from one homeroom made was to perform a poem as a group for extra credit. They had an assignment for their physical education class that required movement. Being inventive, they asked if

FIGURE 5–3. *Ian as Lil Bunny Foo Foo and as a goon at the Poetry Coffeehouse*

they could change the words to a nursery rhyme, and the PE teacher gave them permission. Though this was not the actual English Poetry Coffeehouse assignment, students are often given latitude in adapting assignments as long as they still met the goals for the lesson.

The writer of the new lyrics, Ian, had reinvented the classic nursery rhyme "Little Bunny Foo Foo." The boys created *movements* to a rap battle, much like what is popular on music video channels. This battle pitted Little Bunny Foo Foo (Ian in bunny ears, a white T-shirt, jeans, and a bow tie) against the evil fairy (another boy with wings, a baseball jersey, shorts, and a baseball cap turned to the side). These two both had three other boys serve as *posses* that sang backup by repeating each of the last words that the main characters said in time with the beat, provided by another boy spitting into a microphone. At the end of the poem, the fairy turned Little Bunny Foo Foo into a goon because he had not heeded the fairy's warnings. (See Figure 5–3.)

In the end these boys created a song, memorized it, dressed the part, and performed it in front of hundreds of people, including their parents. They decided to showcase their knowledge of movement, lyrics, music, showmanship, poetry, and, most of all choice, and they brought down the house. (See Figure 5–4.)

Lil Bunny Foo Foo

Lil bunny foo foo hoppin' through the forest (background: forest!)

Pickin up all dem field mice'n bopin dem on da head (background: head!)

Along came a fairy and she didn't look scary but she had a little talk with him and here's what she said (background: said!)

beat beat beat beat beat beat beat beat

Yo! I'm the fairy punk! (background: punk!)

You better stop treatin' them mice like junk (background: junk!)

I'll cast a little spell on you and you'll be a goon

You'll look just like the biggest buffoon

I'll give you two more chances to listen to me

And if you don't you'll regret it so much, you'll see

beat beat beat beat beat beat beat beat

Lil bunny foo foo hoppin' through the forest (background: forest!)

Pickin up all dem field mice'n bopin dem on da head (background: head!)

Along came a fairy and she didn't look scary but she had a little talk with him and here's what she said (background: said!)

beat beat beat beat beat beat beat beat

Yo! I'm the fairy punk! (background: punk!)

You better stop treatin' them mice like junk (background: junk!)

I'll cast a little spell on you and you'll be a goon

You'll look just like the biggest buffoon

I'll give you one more chance to listen to me

And if you don't you'll regret it so much, you'll see

beat beat beat beat beat beat beat beat

Lil bunny foo foo hoppin' through the forest (background: forest!)

Pickin up all dem field mice'n bopin dem on da head (background: head!)

Along came a fairy and she didn't look scary but she had a little talk with him and here's what she said (background: said!)

beat beat beat beat beat beat beat beat

Yo bunny, you got some issues

Gon bust you up so bad them mice'll dis you

Now it's time to turn you into a goon

Them mice'll be laughin' at you pretty soon

beat beat beat beat beat beat beat beat

Lil bunny foo foo learned a great lesson

Them mice aren't the ones you wanna be messin

FIGURE 5–4. *"Lil Bunny Foo Foo" (student rap)*

My coffeehouses have always been ridiculously grand affairs and have gone off so well because of what my school has to offer in terms of facilities, materials, and volunteers. For example, I take over the black box theatre and have an intricate setup with lights, a stage, a sound system, period-appropriate adornments that are created through an interdisciplinary connection to the art department, parent-signed permission slips, jazz music overhead, required costumes, a color program for the parents, videotaping, picture taking of each student during the performance, advanced video and picture CD sales, food, and, of course, coffee. But I know that not all teachers have those resources available at their fingertips.

The nice thing about the coffeehouse is that it can be a classroom presentation and a culminating event after studying poetry at any age. The intimacy of the classroom is perfect for a coffeehouse, allowing the students to literally see each step in the evolution of the word from idea, to the word itself, to its performance. Poetry takes on another life when it is performed, and students deserve that avenue of exploration.

How to Make It Happen

1. The teacher needs to decide on the format and content of the coffeehouse, for these decisions will dictate the assignment's directions. What should the content include? What standards and benchmarks will be utilized? What will the teacher accept as a poem? Should there be a minimum line requirement? Where and when will this event be held? Will the students memorize their poems or have notes? Can students work together?

2. Deadlines must be part of the directions, and these deadlines must leave enough room for students to be assigned a poem if they decide not to turn one in. Assigning a poem is a last resort, but some students drag their feet on purpose so that the teacher will just tell them what to do. Requiring the student to perform the lyrics from Rush's song "Free Will" is an exercise in irony since one line states, "If you choose not to decide, you still have made a choice."

3. Once all of the big questions have been answered, the teacher will write up the directions and hand them out, explaining the entire process.

4. Students then submit three poems to the teacher. Having students turn in more than one poem allows for variety within the coffeehouse as well and helps the class avoid duplicates. This also requires students to read more poetry.

5. After teachers have given students' their chosen poem back, they should impose a deadline for memorization. Teachers can require this by having the students handwrite the poem or perform it, whichever would be most helpful to both parties. The quicker students get off the page, the better performances can become.

6. Students need the time to practice in class often. Obviously teachers will need to balance other curriculum at the same time, but the common rule of thumb is that the closer the coffeehouse date, the more the practice in class is needed.

7. Direct feedback is the best way to allow individual performers and performances to improve. It takes time to see and critique each student, so teachers need to keep this in mind when planning out exactly how much time they will devote to this type of instruction.

8. The setup of the coffeehouse is often patterned after small, dark cafés with candlelight and a small stage, rather than the coffee places students know today, like Starbucks. Depending upon the teacher's vision, available resources, and the number of students presenting, this can be a very detailed scene or a very casual classroom setup.

9. The students need to be given the opportunity to practice in the location of the coffeehouse itself if it will be held outside of the classroom. This allows them to see what they will experience on the day or night of the coffeehouse and give them a mental edge on performing in front of an audience. Telling students about a performance is one thing, but actually walking through the steps of the event can calm many fears. Teachers will need to decide on the order of the participants. Will alphabetical order suffice, or will a genre-by-genre grouping of poems better suit your purposes?

10. Teachers need to plan with parents and volunteers who would like to help with food and drink that will be served at the event.

11. A printed program is essential. Teachers can create an elaborate color program containing advertising or run off a quick ditto with the names of the poems and students to hand out. Teachers need to decide how much time, effort, and money will be put into this activity in advance. Time and the possibility for assistance will determine the available options.

12. The choice of master of ceremonies, or emcee, is particularly important to the success of the show. Turning the reins of a coffeehouse that will be attended by many parents over to students can be tricky at best and a huge mistake at worst. The teacher will need to talk to a student (or students) about the role of the emcee and what will be acceptable

banter and what will not. Some teachers might just want the emcee to say in his or her best announcing voice, "And next up we have ____." Almost every student that has ever been a class clown thinks that he or she has what it takes. Some teachers may want to take the role themselves.

13. After the coffeehouse, the teacher needs to make sure to debrief the entire experience with students. The best ideas for the next year will come from these conversations or written reflections.

The Poetry Coffeehouse offers the most student choice and ownership of any speaking activity in this chapter. Students get to choose the poems they might perform, how they will present the setting, characters, and actions, and how to deliver each line to ensure that the audience will understand their interpretation. Also, the Poetry Coffeehouse provides teachers with a guarantee that students will control the outcome of their presentation and possible success because they own nearly every step of the process.

Adaptations

- Differentiated Instruction: Depending upon the age of the students, specific poetry can be included or excluded. Michael wanted his eighth graders who had already been part of the coffeehouse for the past two years to branch out into more difficult material, so he excluded specific authors to raise the level of possible poetry that could come in.

- Differentiated Instruction: Memorization is close to or completely impossible for some students. If students are required to incorporate a prop into their poetry coffeehouse performance, they may use the prop to keep their lines close to them.

- The classroom itself can be a fine coffeehouse. Construction paper on the windows and a small area in the front of the room surrounded by desks can create the same atmosphere as a big production on a stage with lights, a stage crew, and theatre seating.

- Age-Appropriate Option: A night of Shel Silverstein or any one poet or poetry style is a wonderful coffeehouse option.

- Age-Appropriate Options: The performance of poetry can be done in small groups or even as a whole class. Teachers can give specific lines to individuals and have the entire class memorize the bulk of the poem. The same methods of performance can be used with both small and large groups.

- Interdisciplinary Instruction: Students could be required to find poems from a certain time in history or about a certain subject so that cross-curricular objectives could be strengthened.

Q & A

Why memorize the poem?

When students are required to memorize a poem, they free themselves from the shackles of a script. Movement and voice inflection are that much easier when their hands and mind are free of worry about what that next line is.

Are there any suggestions to help students memorize their poems?

All students have a unique style of learning and memorizing material. One tool that has been very successful in helping students memorize their poems has been to require them to write them out word for word. This works on many levels. The multiple intelligences are tapped when students need to use both verbal/linguistic and visual/spatial means to write and rewrite the text until they memorized it (Kagan and Kagan 1998). Also, students internalize information through KTAV (Kinesthetic, Tactual, Auditory, Visual) activities (Barbe and Milone 1981); having students physically write it, say it as they write it, and see the text emerge on the page as they write it utilizes all three major areas, whether they're writing from memory or copying from the original.

Why does Michael have students submit only poetry from books?

Poetry can be found in many different sources. The Internet has been a warehouse where anyone can write anything and call it a poem. The requirement of poetry that has been published in a book takes those poems that are just floating around in cyberspace out of the mix and adds a feeling of legitimacy to the poems being performed.

Can song lyrics be accepted as poetry?

Yes, by all means!

Have you ever used reader's theatre at the coffeehouse?

Readers theatre is another type of performance that can be adapted to the coffeehouse as a whole. This type of performance requires more stringent rules about being able to interact with characters and could be a great follow-up or lead-in activity to show the different types of performance in action.

Further Resources

Wolf, Allan. 1990. *Something Is Going to Happen: Poetry Performance for the Classroom*. Asheville, NC: Poetry Alive!

———. 1993. *It's Show Time: Poetry from the Page to the Stage*. Asheville, NC: Poetry Alive!

6

Just One More Thing—
An End with a Bang!

Each of the activities described in the preceding chapters has played a part in enabling our students the opportunity to choose. Each activity is designed to place students in the driver's seat of their education, and all of the personal experience stories, step-by-step directions, adaptations, questions and answers, and references work together as resources for teachers to help students know where they can drive. Without the teacher, however, students fumble around in the dark, looking for the car keys, just dying for the chance to take a spin downtown on a crisp, fall night in the convertible of their dreams.

In the same vein as each of the past activities, we would like to wrap up with an activity that could be added to just about any of the previous ones. It is aptly titled Just One More Thing.

Just One More Thing

Michael has always tried to give assignments that make students think, but for a while, students were turning in some very bland products, until he decided to add Just One More Thing, a device he learned from Jeff Golub at the University of South Florida.

When looking back at the recipe of all those bland products, he noticed that there seemed to be some ingredient that was missing that could make the resulting meal spectacular. Adding Just One More Thing to the recipe turned the bland into a culinary delight.

Truthfully, assignments that had this added dash of vagueness originally infuriated Michael because they were too open-ended. Upon further internalization, however, he realized the assignments that required Michael to look deeper were the first assignments that allowed for open interpretation, and any supported and reasonable answer that still followed all of the directions was accepted. Back in his own classroom, he added a specific but nebulous requirement onto the end of some of his assignments, and his students began to rethink how they turned in assignments, which brought a new vigor to their work.

Michael's Experience

The I Am poem has been a favorite activity of mine for a long time, usually employed at the beginning of the year as a get-to-know-you assignment in which the students tell about themselves. Sometimes we do a We Are poem as a community-building experience to characterize a new class' identity and include some goals for the class as a whole. A copy of a blank I Am poem can be found on the Internet with relative ease, since the original work is long out of print.

When I decided to use the I Am poem as a test for the summer reading book *To Kill a Mockingbird* (TKAM), I originally wrote these directions: "Write an I Am poem by taking on the persona of either Scout, Boo, Tom, or Mayella. You must include details from the book, characterization, and references to both theme and symbolism."

After students had completed a plethora of assignments on theme, character, point of view, plot, symbolism, and language over a four-week period, I thought they would appreciate a creative outlet for their final assessment of the book, and I saw the I Am poem as that outlet. It turned out that students looked at that last assignment of the TKAM unit as yet another exercise with requirements, and I got back exactly what I asked for: I Am poems from the point of view of one of the four characters that followed the format, utilized required elements, and were completely devoid of feeling, life, and personality.

The following year I reevaluated the I Am poem test, and an overwhelming feeling of dread came over me. I still really liked the idea, but I wanted to improve it. I wanted the students to be challenged and excited about it, to embrace it instead of just do it. I decided to keep all of the same requirements, but then I added Just One More Thing. I added a requirement that stated, "You must make your test meaningful."

I wanted to know how the students would react. Would they give me something more? More importantly, I felt that, by adding this nonspecific requirement and then letting the students have the choice to interpret it for themselves individually, the blah assignments of the previous year would be less prevalent.

I am scared and lonely
I wonder how I can get myself out of this situation
I hear the voices in my head telling me to state the truth
I see everyone staring strait into my eyes as I convict an innocent black man
I want to leave my family and live on my own
I am scared and lonely

I pretend to love my father
I feel violated by the actions of my father
I touch my bruised cheek that I got from my father
I worry about the consequences Tom will have for my selfish lying
I cry that I have to lie for the sake of my father's reputation
I am scared and lonely

I understand that I am doing something wrong
I say that Tom Robinson raped me but really it was my father
I dream of a way to make this all go away
I try to say that my fathers at fault but I am distracted by his devilish stare
I hope that everything will turn out okay
I am scared and lonely

FIGURE 6–1. *Amy's TKAM I Am Poem Test*

And it worked!

Students did balk at the test at first because of its seemingly overwhelming options. How could they possibly choose what would make the test meaningful? Meaningful to whom? Them? The teacher? The rest of the class? They demanded examples. They demanded clarification, but I stayed steadfast and gave the same answer each time: "You have all of the directions you need to make clear choices for your assignment. Be able to explain your reasoning behind your choices."

And it worked!

Amy created a meaningful project with a copy of her poem and a piece of bright orange poster board. She rolled up the poster into a six-inch wide tube and taped her poem onto one end so that the reader had to look through the tube to see the poem (Figure 6–1).

When looking at the tube as it stood upright, a student would see that Amy had cut the top of the tube and made it into a pointed and jagged opening. As it stood on a desk, students could look into the tube and read the poem, but the poem did not have a title or a specific character name within it. When asked whom the poem was about, Amy would smile and say, "Hold it up to the light."

Amy had created an amazing poem, but she also had created a metaphor. To look at the situation and this character, a student had to be careful not to cut herself on the jagged opening. This physically depicted the harshness and callousness of Tom Robinson's trial and eventual conviction. When students picked up the tube and lifted it to the light, they saw the name of Tom's accuser, the lying, deceitful, and lonely Mayella. Amy had ever-so-lightly penciled in her name onto the poem, but students could not see her name until they lifted the poem to the light, shining the light of justice and truth on the person who had the hardest time being truthful throughout the novel.

Ingenious? Yes!

Meaningful? Absolutely!

Lynne created another amazing embodiment of meaning. She took a fence post and attached branches of fake leaves to it. She then wrote her poem about Boo Radley on her makeshift tree. When asked why she had put her test together in this way, she explained that Boo was a mockingbird because although he was made to hide away in his house, he desperately wanted to play and sing with Jem and Scout. He used the tree's knothole to communicate until his father sealed it up. Placing the poem about Boo on a tree gave him the freedom to sing and be heard.

Ingenious? Yes!

Meaningful? Absolutely!

Adding Just One More Thing to this test transformed it from just another assignment to an opportunity for something more. Opening the door of creativity and possibility is the best gift I have ever given to my students.

How to Make It Happen

1. Teachers must look at their curriculum and choose any assignment or test that needs a jump start. Sure it works fine right now, but what might it become?

2. Teachers must then decide what will become the last requirement of the assignment, Just One More Thing. Interestingly enough, the assignment may already have this Just One More Thing requirement within it. Sometimes within the assignment, the directions tell students to be thorough, descriptive, or reflective, but that becomes

embedded in the directions and gets lost. It needs a more prominent position; make it that one important last requirement of the assignment.

3. Teachers then need to set up the directions of the assignment in such a way that this special requirement sticks out. Descriptive assignments could include the directions "Make this assignment visually appealing to a blind man." Reflective assignments could include "Make this assignment all about your life outside of school or all about you and your friends."

Adaptations

- Teachers have the option of offering a grading rubric ahead of time that further clarifies the assignment as a whole or clearly identifies the parameters for their Just One More Thing. This may take some of the guesswork and vagueness out of the assignment, concretizing a concept instead of leaving it completely open.
- A Writing Option: "Make the story creepy/disturbing/surprising/startling/amazing/miraculous/comically mysterious."
- A Writing Option: "Make the story have a twist of fate/an ironic turn of events/a paranoid delusion/a heart-pounding conclusion."
- A Writing Option: Through a two-person conversation, readers must learn a secret. This writing assignment would be entirely made up of dialogue between two characters. Readers would be able to easily understand the action and setting of the story as well as the relationship between the characters. This could be in the form of
    1. instant messaging on a computer screen
    2. a phone conversation
    3. a personal conversation

    Teachers could give students the above prompt and then tell them that the conversation can be on any topic or even one of the following: a conversation about breaking up, a confession, someone dying, someone winning the lottery, someone who has a crush, and so on.
- A Writing Option: Teachers can create a writing assignment with a specific word count requirement, such as 100, 78, or 165 words, which forces students to learn the economy of language.
- A Writing Option: Teachers could ask students to write a response to poetry by creating poetry that is dynamic/devilish/grandiose/picayune/playful/undulating/arduous/arcane.

- A Writing Option: Teachers could ask students to write a response to a novel that is completely outrageous/irritating/outlandish/over-the-top/flabbergasting/tempting/ticklish/curt.
- Just One More Thing can be as simple as "Impress me with your creativity" or "Make your audience say, 'Wow!'"

APPENDIX
91 WAYS TO RESPOND TO A BOOK

This is the original list of ninety-one ways to respond to books, offered by Anne Arvidson on an NCTE listserv in the early 1990s.

1. **Write the story in the book from a different point of view.** Take an entire story (or part of it) and write a version as someone else would tell it.

2. **Write the diary a main character might have written.** Imagine you are the person in your book. Write a diary for a few days or weeks as she or he would have done.

3. **Write a character sketch of someone in the book.** This might be the central character or a minor supporting character in the story. Tell what he looked like, but also include favorite color, horoscope sign, sports liked, and even a bumper-sticker or a T-shirt.

4. **Rearrange a passage as a "found" poem.** Find a particularly effective description or bit of action that is really poetry written as prose. Rewrite it. Leave out words or skip a sentence or two, but arrange it to create a poem.

5. **Write a parody of the book.** This kind of humorous imitation appeals to many students. Parody the entire book or one scene.

6. **Write a promotion campaign for a movie about the book.** This could include newspaper ad layouts, radio and television commercials, and any special events.

7. **Write a letter to the author of the book.** While authors may not have time to respond to each letter they receive, they do enjoy letters from their readers—especially those that discuss the books in the reader's own terms. Send letters in care of the book publishers if you cannot locate the author's address in *Who's Who, Current Biography,* or other reference sources.

8. **Put together a cast for the film version of a book.** Imagine the director-producer wants a casting director to make recommendations. Decide who would be the actors and actresses. Include photos and descriptions of the stars and tell why each is "perfect" for the part. Write a report to convince the producer of the selections.

9. **Write a report of related information about one topic or person in the book.** For example, research information about the trial of Benedict Arnold, how the covered wagons traveled, fishing off a particular island, and so on.

10. **Make a new book jacket.** It should include an attractive picture or cover design, an original summary of the book, information on the author and illustrator, and information about other books by the author.

11. **Convert a book to a radio drama.** Give a live or taped version about the story—or a scene from it—as a radio play. Include an announcer and sound effects.

12. **Do a dramatic reading (reader's theatre) of a scene.** Select the scene and ask friends to help read it dramatically.

13. **Convert a book into a puppet show.** Make simple puppets (stick puppets, finger puppets, paper bag puppets, and so on) or complex puppets (marionettes) and present the story or an exciting scene from it.

14. **Do a "you are there" news program**, reporting on a particular scene, character, or event in the book.

15. **Write and stage a television series episode.** Think of a popular television series that a book or part of it would fit. Then convert it to that series and give the segment before the class.

16. **Prepare a television commercial about a book.** Imagine a book is the basis for a miniseries on television. Prepare and give the television commercials that would make people want to watch it.

17. **Use body masks and present a scene from your book.** Make full-sized cardboard figures with cutouts for the face and hands. Use them to dramatize the scene.

18. **Dramatize a scene from a book with other students taking parts.** If desired, use props and costumes. If the students know the story, improvise the scripts.

19. **Play Charades based on various books members of the class have read.** Review standard charade signals. Divide into teams. Then have the students draw titles of books or the names of characters in the books, concentrating on those that have been most popular.

20. **Make a soap or paraffin carving about an event or person in a book.** These are inexpensive materials and soft enough so there is little danger from the tools used for carving.

21. **Mold plaster relief designs.** Pour plaster into a form over various objects and then antique or shellac them to make interesting displays.

22. **Make life-sized paper-stuffed animals, people, or objects found in a book.** Cut out two large sheets of wrapping paper in the shape desired. Staple the edges almost all the way around. Stuff with crumpled newspaper, finish stapling, and paint.

23. **Make hand looms and weavings that portray a design in a book.** Almost anything—from paper plates to forked sticks—will make a loom when strung with yarn, rope, or cord. Check art and craft books for directions. Then use the creations as wall hangings or mobiles.

24. **Create batik designs with wax and old sheets of tie-dye material.** When dry and ironed, use them for wall hangings, curtains, and costumes.

25. **Fashion a mobile from items related to a story.** The mobiles add color and movement to a room. Display them in the library, the cafeteria, the multipurpose room, or in the hallway.

26. **Make a "roll-movie" of the scenes or events of a book.** Put a series of pictures in sequence on a long strip of paper. Attach ends to rollers and place in a cardboard box. Print simple dialogue to accompany the frames.

27. **Make an animation of a scene on an adding machine tape.** To get animation, draw a sequence of pictures with each one showing a bit more movement than the preceding one. When this is rolled quickly, it gives the appearance of motion.

28. **Create filmstrips of a story.** Commercially produced materials are available with special colored pens to make filmstrips.

29. **Print a design from a story in a book using a variety of materials.** Here, too, the process may be simple or complicated. Use potatoes or other raw vegetables to carve and use. Or try plastic meat trays and silk-screen prints.

30. **Impersonate a character and tell an episode in a book.** Dress up as a character and retell the story.

31. **Discuss the book informally with one or two other students.** The reader should choose two people he or she thinks might enjoy the book. Find a quiet corner to talk about it.

32. **Interview a character from a book.** Prepare questions to give another student. The reader assumes the role of the character in the book and answers the questions as that character.

33. **Conduct a small group discussion.** Several students who have read a particular book should get together and discuss it.

34. **Focus a discussion about a particular person.** Compare biographies of characters in historical fiction.

35. **Compare versions of the same story.** Contrast different versions of one story or several stories with similar themes.

36. **Have a panel or roundtable discussion on the same topic.** Use one of the bibliographies of books on a particular topic (death, loneliness, handicaps, heroes and heroines, and so on). Have the group present summaries of their books.

37. **Pitch a sales talk for a book.** Give everyone in the class tokens, play money, or straw votes. After the sales talk, take bids to get the most for the book.

38. **Interview a book's author.** The reader becomes the author and comes to visit the class, who in turn interviews him or her.

39. **Portray a book character.** Ask another reader of the same book to role-play a different character. The two characters can meet to talk about themselves and what has happened to them. This is especially appropriate if they have something in common: similar adventures, similar jobs, and so on.

40. **Make a talking display of a book.** Tape a dialogue or description about an event, scene, or character.

41. **Draw a scale model of an item in a story.** Making an object from the story to scale presents many challenges. For example, try a go-cart, a matchlock gun, or any other item.

42. **Cook a food mentioned in your book.** It is always fun to share something to eat. Please cook your recipe at home.

43. **Build a relief map of the setting of the story.** Use clay, sand, or papier-mâché.

44. **Design and make your own T-shirt of an illustration about a book.** Create a design, using colorfast marking pens.

45. **Construct a building from a story.** Work together with others to build an item from the story that they have read also.

46. **Make some costume dolls for a display of characters in a book.** Create costume dolls and display them.

47. **Complete scale drawings of rooms in a book.** Use graph paper with a set scale and design places portrayed in a book.

48. **Learn to play a game mentioned in a book.** Teach it to the rest of the class. (This might be an old-fashioned game or one from another country.)

49. **Ask others in the class to design and create squares for a quilt.** Depict favorite scenes or characters, then stitch/draw/paint the quilt together. The individual squares may be drawn with marking pens or

done in stitches. The quilt may be a wall hanging, a curtain for a private reading area in the room, or presented to the school as a class gift.

50. **Convert the events of a story into a ballad or song.** Write the lyrics and music or adapt words to a melody by someone else.

51. **Make a literary map of the author's works and life.** Use references, biographical, and autobiographical materials (articles, books, interviews) to create an informative and colorful map.

52. **Invent word games for your book.** Create crossword puzzles, word games, and acrostics incorporating unfamiliar vocabulary words, characters, and settings. Distribute to the class.

53. **Compare lifestyles.** As a group project, have the students compare the way of life in the book to present-day living in their community. This can be presented in panel format. For example, the methods of transportation, fashions, foods, customs, religious practices, types of government can be compared to their modern counterparts.

54. **Group performance.** Select a crucial scene from the novel and have the members of the group perform the scene. Have one member interrupt it, posing as a reporter. Have him/her interview each character for an on-the-scene "mini-cam" report.

55. **The written word versus the video.** Compare the book to the movie or television version of it. What aspects of the book have been altered for the visual performance and why? Do these alterations make the story "better"? Why or why not?

56. **The novel outside the English class.** Show how a historical novel could be used in a history class or how a science fiction novel could enliven a science course.

57. **Return to the future.** Pretend that you are one of the characters who has returned 25 years after the novel has ended. Describe your reactions.

58. **Write or act out a telephone conversation between two of the characters.**

59. **Novel court.** Hold a "mock trial" to permit one of the characters to defend what he has done in some controversial scene in the book. Let members of the class deliberate as the jury and arrive at a verdict.

60. **Silent plays.** Have a group of students pantomime a scene from the book. Give special attention to movement and facial expressions to convey the meaning of the scene.

61. **Write a short playlet based on some character or event in the story.** Be sure to provide accurate and interesting stage directions.

62. **Personal taste.** Select one character from the book. If he/she were living today, what kind of clothes, books, records, movies, etc. would he/she select? Why would he/she do so?

63. **Design the front page of a newspaper.** Write a short news story describing the major event in your book. Include an attention grabbing headline and teasers for the rest of the paper.

64. **Write a human interest story on one of the characters in the story.**

65. **Write an editorial on some controversial issue raised by the book.**

66. **Design a comic strip retelling some event in the story.** This may be expanded to tell the whole story of the novel as a comic book.

67. **Design a children's story retelling some event in the story.** This may be expanded to tell the whole story of the novel as a children's book.

68. **Design a time line for the events in the story.**

69. **Design a detailed map or maps for the setting(s) of the book.**

70. **Design a bulletin board to stimulate class interest in the book.**

71. **Write a legend, fable, or myth based on some event in the story.**

72. **Pen some poetry.** Write a limerick or a short poem about one of the characters or some event in the novel.

73. **Write a ballad and/or music telling the story.** This can be delivered or sung to the class.

74. **Create an eye-catching poster.** Choose a scene from the book and cast it in a poster that would attract potential readers or buyers to the book.

75. **Fiction or reality.** Choose a character that seems to have realistic experiences. Write about something similar that has happened to you.

76. **Function as an editor.** Treat the book as a manuscript and rewrite the pages (or chapter) you consider "weak." What needs to be redone to make the book stronger?

77. **Trading places.** Write a short paper explaining why you would or would not like to change places with one of the characters in the novel.

78. **Design the illustrations for the book.**

79. **Write a personal letter to one of the characters you admire or despise.**

80. **Correspond with another character.** Pretend that you are one character in the book. Write a friendly letter to another character.

81. **Character in search of a job.** As if you were a character in the book, compose a resume and cover letter for your character, who is applying for a job suitable for the character and the setting of the novel. Does your character have any references?

82. **Once upon a time.** Write a fairy tale about some event or character in the book.

83. **Be a modern artist.** Using various mediums, create a collage that comments on a particular theme or issue in the book.

84. **Create a dossier on a character.** Pretend that you are a foreign spy sent to report on your chosen character. Compile secret files, general and specific information regarding your character. Don't forget the photo.

85. **Design and produce a postcard or a series of postcards.** On one side draw/paint/reproduce an appropriate photo and on the other side compose a message to me from one of the characters. There will be automatic As for the best design, most intriguing message, most distant postmark, and most appropriate postmark (mail it to me from there!).

86. **Publish a yearbook.** Create a yearbook—alias annual, alias class book, alias memory book—based on the people and events in your book. Refer to a real yearbook for ideas on layout and sections.

87. **Be a literary agent.** Pretend you are a literary agent representing the author of your book. Write to Harry Decision, editor of young adult fiction at Bantam Books, explaining why you feel he should publish your author's book.

88. **Compile a scrapbook or a memory box.** Choose one of the major characters in your book, and, as that person, put together a scrapbook or memory box of special memories and mementos. Be true to your character.

89. **Design a travel brochure.** Illustrate and advertise the "world" of your novel.

90. **The fortune cookie review.** Explain why their messages, given to each of the novel's characters, are amazingly appropriate.

91. **The edible (chocolate?) review.** Sir Francis Bacon said, "Some books are to be tasted, others to be swallowed, and some to be chewed and digested."

WORKS CITED

Arvidson, Anne J. 2004. 91 Ways to Respond to Literature. NCTE Talk, August 24.

Atwell, Nancie. 1987. *In the Middle: Writing, Reading, and Learning with Adolescents*. Portsmouth, NH: Boynton/Cook.

———. 2003. "Hard Trying and These Recipes." *English Journal* 11 (2): 16–19.

Barbe, Walter B., and Michael N. Milone Jr. 1981. "What We Know About Modality Strengths." *Educational Leadership* 38 (5): 378–80.

Beers, Kylene, and Robert E. Probst. 2004. Teaching Struggling Readers; Teaching Readers to Struggle. Speech presented at the annual National Council of Teachers of English Conference, Indianapolis, IN, November 19.

Bigelow, Terry P., and Michael J. Vokoun. 2005. "Stepping into the Classroom." *English Journal* 94 (4): 115–20.

Blau, Sheridan. 2001. "Politics and the English Language Arts." In *The Fate of Progressive Language Policies and Practices*, edited by C. Dudley-Marling and C. Edelsky, 183–208. Urbana, IL: NCTE.

Burke, Jim. 2001. *Illuminating Texts: How to Teach Students to Read the World*. Portsmouth, NH: Heinemann.

Calkins, Lucy M. 1983. *Lessons from a Child*. Portsmouth, NH: Boynton/Cook.

———. 1986. *The Art of Teaching Writing*. Portsmouth, NH: Boynton/Cook.

———. 1991. *Living Between the Lines*. Portsmouth, NH: Boynton/Cook.

Collins, Billy. 2003. "Introduction to Poetry." In *Poetry 180*. New York: Random House.

Cook, Reginald. 1974. *Robert Frost: A Living Voice*. Amherst: University of Massachusetts Press.

Dewey, John. 1990. *The School and Society and the Child and the Curriculum*. Chicago: University of Chicago Press.

Dudley-Marling, Curt. 1995. "Complicating Ownership." In *Who Owns Learning? Questions of Autonomy, Choice, and Control*, edited by C. Dudley-Marling and D. Searle, 1–15. Portsmouth, NH: Heinemann.

Freire, Paulo. 1973. *Education for Critical Consciousness*. New York: Seabury.

Gardner, Howard E. 1993. *Frames of Mind: The Theory of Multiple Intelligences*. New York: Basic Books.

Golub, Jeffrey N. 1994. *Activities for an Interactive Classroom*. Urbana, IL: NCTE.

———. 2000. *Making Learning Happen: Strategies for an Interactive Classroom*. Portsmouth, NH: Boynton/Cook.

Goodman, Ken. 1986. *What's Whole in Whole Language?* Richmond Hill, Ontario: Scholastic-TAB.

Graves, Donald. 1983. *Writing: Teachers and Children at Work.* Portsmouth, NH: Boynton/Cook.

International Baccalaureate Organization. n.d. IBO Mission Statement. www.ibo.org/ibo/index.cfm?page=/ibo/about&language=EN (accessed December 28, 2004).

Kagan, Spencer, and Miguel Kagan. 1998. *Multiple Intelligences: The Complete Book.* San Clemente, CA: Kagan Cooperative Learning.

Kilpatrick, William H. 1918. "The Project Method." *Teacher's College Record* (September): 319–35.

Kohn, Alfie. 1998. *What to Look for in a Classroom . . . and Other Essays.* Hoboken, NJ: Jossey-Bass.

Macrorie, Ken. 1988. *The I-Search Paper.* Portsmouth, NH: Heinemann.

Mahoney, Jim. 2002. *Power and Portfolios: Best Practices for High School Classrooms.* Portsmouth, NH: Heinemann.

Moffett, James. 1983. *Teaching the Universe of Discourse.* Boston: Houghton Mifflin.

Preller, Paula. 2004. "Fostering Thoughtful Literacy in Elementary Classrooms." Center on English Learning and Achievement. http://cela.albany.edu/newslet /spring00/fostering.htm (accessed December 12, 2004).

Probst, Robert E. 1988. *Response and Analysis: Teaching Literature in Junior and Senior High School.* Portsmouth, NH: Heinemann.

Rief, Linda. 1992. *Seeking Diversity.* Portsmouth, NH: Heinemann.

Roller, Cathy M., ed. 2001. *Learning to Teach Reading: Setting the Research Agenda.* Newark, DE: International Reading Association.

Rosenblatt, Louise M. 1938. *Literature as Exploration.* New York: Appleton-Century-Crofts.

Short, Kathy G. 1997. "Inquiring into Inquiry: Is It More of the Same or Something Quite New?" *Learning* 25 (6): 55–57.

Smith, Dora V. 1964. *Dora V. Smith: Selected Essays.* New York: Macmillan.

Smith, Michael W., and Jeffrey D. Wilhelm. 2002. *Reading Don't Fix No Chevys: Literacy in the Lives of Young Men.* Portsmouth, NH: Heinemann.

Todd, Catherine. 1995. *The Semester Project: The Power and Pleasures of Independent Study.* Urbana, IL: English Journal.

Tovani, Cris. 2000. *I Read It, but I Don't Get It: Comprehension Strategies for Adolescent Readers.* Portland, ME: Stenhouse.

Wilhelm, Jeffrey. 2003. Reading in the Contact Zone: Using Symbolic Story Representation, Art, and Drama to Support Reading and Thinking About Reading. Speech presented at the annual National Council of Teachers of English Conference, San Francisco, November 22.

———. 2004a. Middle Level Get Together. Speech presented at the annual National Council of Teachers of English Conference, Indianapolis, IN, November 18.

———. 2004b. *Reading IS Seeing: Learning to Visualize Scenes, Characters, Ideas, and Text Worlds to Improve Comprehension and Reflective Reading.* New York: Scholastic.

INDEX

Moffett, James, xiii
Multiple intelligences (MI), 42, 66, 103, 145

National Council of Teachers of English (NCTE), viii, ix, 2, 38
Night (Wiesel), 17
91 Ways to Respond to a Book (Arvidson), 38, 153–59
No More Dead Dogs (Korman), 44

Odyssey (Homer), 94, 95, 96, 101, 102
Old Man and the Sea, The (Hemingway), 81
Open Mind activity, 23
Oral communication. *See* Speaking
Oral practice, 143
Outsiders, The (Hinton), 17, 18, 30
Ownership, vii, 2, 10, 34, 35, 67, 73, 77, 79, 118

Parents
   communication with, 69, 73, 75
Peart, Neil, xi
Pet Semetary (King), xvii
Poetry Alive, 135
Portfolios in the Writing Classroom: An Introduction (Blake Yancey), 93
Power and Portfolios: Best Practices for High School Classrooms (Mahoney), 93
Power of Three, 107–108
Preller, Paula, 8
Probst, Robert E., 7, 20
Public speaking. *See* Speaking

Reader, the Text, and the Poem: The Transactional Theory of the Literary Work, The (Rosenblatt), 22
Reader response, 15, 30, 34
Reading
   outside, 74
   reluctant, 30

"Reading Don't Fix No Chevys": Literacy in the Lives of Young Men (Smith and Wilhelm), 4
Reading IS Seeing: Learning to Visualize Scenes, Characters, Ideas, and Text Worlds, to Improve Comprehension and Reflective Reading (Wilhelm), 13, 18, 29
Reflection, by students, 77, 91
Response and Analysis: Teaching Literature in Junior and Senior High School (Probst), 20
Revision, 109
Rhapsode, 95, 97, 101
Rief, Linda, 82, 86, 87, 128
Riekehof, Lottie L., 39
Role playing, 107
Rosenblatt, Louise, 3, 22, 56
Rubrics. *See* Assessment
Rush, xi

Seeking Diversity (Rief), 82, 86
Setting, 82, 104, 111, 139
Shoeless Joe (Kinsella), xix
Short, Kathy G., 8
Small group. *See* Cooperative learning
Smith, Dora V., 2
Smith, Michael W., 7
Speaking, fear of public, 120, 122, 124, 125, 131, 143
Specific learning disorder (SLD), xviii
Standardized tests, 67
Stellaluna (Cannon), xvii,
"Stopping by Woods on a Snowy Evening" (Frost), 48
Strickland, Jim, ix
Symbolism, 31, 35

Tampa Bay Area Writing Project (TBAWP), 107
Tampa Museum of Art, 113
To Kill a Mockingbird (Lee), 148
Todd, Catherine, 1